OSPREY MILITARY · **CAMPAIGN SERIES** · 24

ARNHEM 1944

GENERAL EDITOR DAVID G. CHANDLER

OSPREY MILITARY

CAMPAIGN SERIES 24

ARNHEM 1944

OPERATION 'MARKET GARDEN'

STEPHEN BADSEY

◀ *Paratroops of British
1st Parachute Brigade
landing on Drop Zone 'X'
near Wolheze, just west of
Arnhem, 1353 local time,
Sunday 17 September
1944, taken from an RAF
reconnaissance Spitfire. A
three-man team from the
Army Film and Photo-
graphic Unit, together
with newspaper reporters
and a BBC radio team,
landed with 1st British
Airborne Division to
cover the battle. (IWM
photograph CL1168)*

▼ *Arnhem town centre, taken looking southeast towards the road bridge by a Mosquito of RAF 2 Group, 2nd Tactical Air Force, during the preliminary bombing of German defences in the* *'Market-Garden' area on the morning of Sunday 17 September. The embanked section of roadway and the houses on the north side of the road bridge formed the site of Lieutenant Colonel* *Frost's defence. The flat ground to the south across the river was the planned landing site for 1st Polish Parachute Brigade. (IWM photograph CL1201)*

First published in 1993 by Osprey, an imprint of Reed Consumer Books Limited, Michelin House, 81 Fulham Road, London SW3 6RB and Auckland, Melbourne, Singapore and Toronto

© Copyright 1993 Reed International Books Limited
Reprinted 1994

ISBN 1-85532-302-8

For a catalogue of all books published by Osprey Military please write to:

The Marketing Manager, Consumer Catalogue Department, Osprey Publishing Ltd, Michelin House, 81 Fulham Road, London SW3 6RB

Key to Map Symbols

Army Group		Infantry
Army		Cavalry
Corps		Artillery
Division		Armour
Brigade		Motorized
Regiment		Airborne
Battalion		Special Forces

CONTENTS

Prints credited to the IWM are available on application from the Department of Photographs, Imperial War Museum, Lambeth Road, London SE1 6HZ. All other prints are from the collection of Brian L. Davis. The author is grateful to both for their help with this book.

THE ORIGINS OF THE BATTLE

The Battle of Arnhem, known by its Allied codename of Operation 'Market-Garden', was the largest airborne battle in history, and the only attempt in the Second World War by the Allies to use airborne troops in a strategic role in Europe. It was a battle of Army Groups numbering hundreds of thousands of men – 21st Army Group under Field Marshal Sir Bernard Montgomery against Army Group B under Generalfeldmarschall Walther Model – but repeatedly its outcome hinged on the actions of small forces and individual battalions at crucial points. Rather than a set-piece battle with a tidy beginning and end, it began on 17 September 1944 from a confused and daily changing pattern of events, and ended ten days later as the only major defeat of Montgomery's career, and the only Allied defeat in the campaign in North-West Europe.

The direct origin of the Battle of Arnhem was actually Montgomery's greatest victory, the Battle of Normandy (described in *Normandy 1944: Allied Landings and Breakout*, Campaigns Series 1). The destruction of the original Army Group B (Seventh Army and Fifth Panzer Army) in the Falaise Pocket in August 1944 at the end of the battle was a disaster for Adolf Hitler's Third Reich. Of 38 German divisions committed to Normandy, 25 were completely destroyed, with at least 240,000 men killed or wounded, and a further 200,000 taken prisoner. Generalfeldmarschall Model, appointed on 18 August as both Commander-in-Chief West (Oberbefelshaber West or OB West) and commander of Army Group B, found himself managing the rout of his shattered forces across northern France into Belgium and Holland.

In the planning before D-Day on 6 June, the Allies had assumed that they would advance steadily inland, with General Dwight D. Eisenhower, commanding Supreme Headquarters Allied Expeditionary Forces (SHAEF), taking over the land

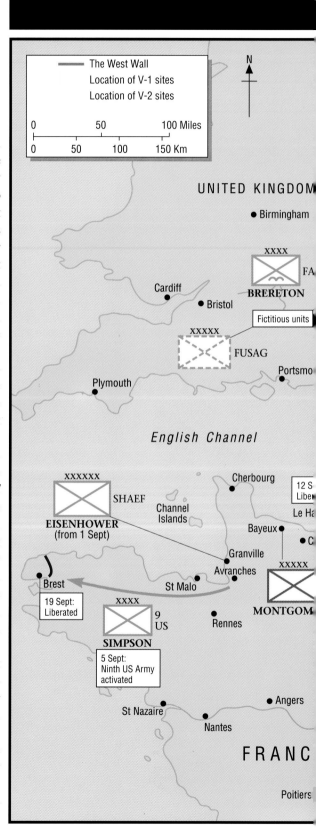

The Allied Pursuit, 26 August to 10 September 1944

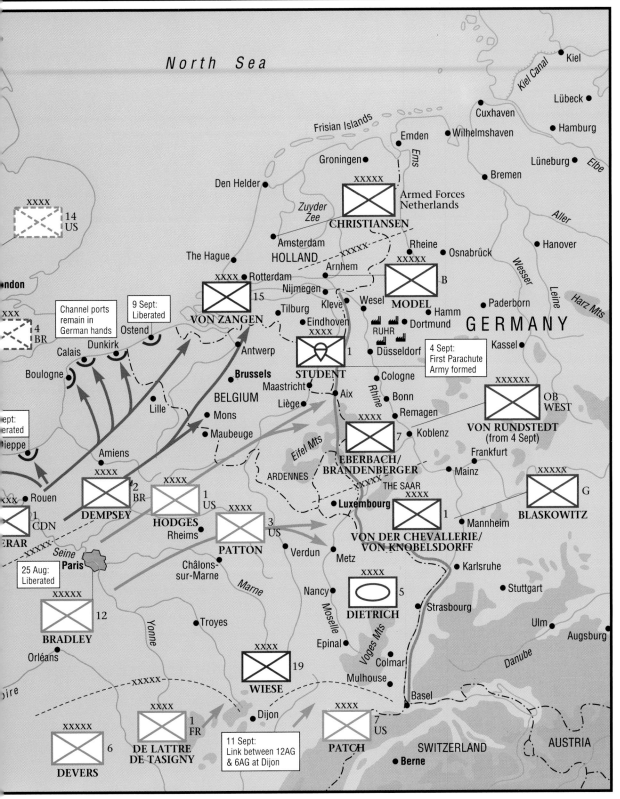

North Sea

Kiel

Kiel Canal

Lübeck

Cuxhaven

Hamburg

Emden • Wilhelmshaven

Frisian Islands

Ems

Lüneburg *Elbe*

Bremen

Groningen

Den Helder

XXXXX
CHRISTIANSEN

Armed Forces
Netherlands

Hanover

Aller

*Zuyder
Zee*

HOLLAND

Rheine

Osnabrück

XXXXX

Wesser

XXXX
14
US

Amsterdam

The Hague

XXXXX

Arnhem

Leine

Harz Mts

XXXX
15
VON ZANGEN

Rotterdam
Nijmegen
Tilburg

Wesel
Kleve

XXXXX
B
MODEL

Paderborn

GERMANY

ndon

XXX
4
BR

Channel ports
remain in
German hands

9 Sept:
Liberated

Ostend

Eindhoven
Antwerp

Hamm
Dortmund

RUHR

XXXX
1
STUDENT

Düsseldorf

Kassel

4 Sept:
First Parachute
Army formed

Calais
Dunkirk

Boulogne

Lille

Brussels

BELGIUM

Maastricht

Liège

Aix

Cologne

Bonn

Remagen

Rhine

XXXXXX
OB
WEST
VON RUNDSTEDT
(from 4 Sept)

ept:
erated

ieppe

Mons
Maubeuge

Eifel Mts

XXXX
7

Koblenz

Frankfurt

VON DER CHEVALLERIE/
VON KNOBELSDORFF

Mainz

Amiens

ARDENNES

EBERBACH/
BRANDENBERGER

XXXXX
G
BLASKOWITZ

XXXX
2
BR
DEMPSEY

Rouen

XXXX
1
US
HODGES
Rheims

XXXXX

THE SAAR

XXXX
1

Mannheim

Karlsruhe

XXX
1
CDN

XXXX
3
US
PATTON

Luxembourg

Verdun

Metz

Stuttgart

ERAR

Seine

25 Aug:
Liberated

Paris

Châlons-
sur-Marne

Nancy

XXXX
5
DIETRICH

Strasbourg

Ulm

Augsburg

XXXXX
12
BRADLEY

Marne

Troyes

Yonne

Epinal

Moselle

Voges Mts

Colmar

Danube

Orléans

oire

XXXX
19
WIESE

Mulhouse

Basel

XXXXX
6
DEVERS

XXXX
1
FR
DE LATTRE
DE TASIGNY

Dijon

11 Sept:
Link between 12AG
& 6AG at Dijon

XXXX
7
US
PATCH

SWITZERLAND

Berne

AUSTRIA

7

▶ *As part of the creation of First Allied Airborne Army, Major General Matthew Ridgway of the 82nd ('All American') Airborne Division was promoted to command the new US XVIII Airborne Corps and succeeded by his deputy, Brigadier General James 'Slim Jim' Gavin. This picture shows the handover ceremony on 10 August. Left to right on the saluting base are Gavin, Eisenhower, Ridgway and Brereton, who is still wearing his 9th Air Force shoulder patch.*

▲ *General Eisenhower with the senior officers of Bradley's 12th Army Group, taken in May 1945 at the end of the war in Europe. Front row left to right are Lieutenant General William H Simpson commanding Ninth US Army, Patton, General Carl Spaatz commanding US Strategic and Tactical Air Forces, Eisenhower, Bradley, Hodges, and Lieutenant General*

Leonard T. Gerow, commanding Fifteenth US Army (not formed in September 1944). Standing between Eisenhower and Bradley is Lieutenant General Walter Bedell Smith, Eisenhower's chief of staff, and next to him (with peaked cap) is Lieutenant General Hoyt S. Vandenberg, who replaced Brereton commanding 9th Air Force on 7 August 1944.

battle from Montgomery after a few weeks and directing the advance of his three Army Groups – Montgomery's 21st Army Group, 12th Army Group under Lieutenant General Omar Bradley, and 6th Army Group under Lieutenant General Jacob Devers coming from southern France – on a broad front against a strong German defence. Instead, the Battle of Normandy had been weeks of hard-fought virtual stalemate followed by a sudden German collapse resulting in the Falaise pocket.

The very size of this victory was Montgomery's undoing. Success in Normandy had depended on cooperation between the various Allied members and services. Now, with the unexpected destruction

of Army Group B, many on both sides believed that history was repeating itself, and that August 1944 in France was August 1918 once more, with Germany virtually defeated and bound to surrender before the year ended. Senior Allied commanders, taught to regard a successful war as just one episode in their developing careers, began to display openly the self-interest and concern for their own futures they had kept buried during the battle.

After some delay, Eisenhower was due to assume command from Montgomery on 1 September, establishing SHAEF Headquarters at Granville in western Normandy. On 13 August, as Army Group B's encirclement was being completed, Montgomery first raised with Eisenhower the idea of changing Allied strategy to a 'single thrust' advance by his own 21st Army Group, supported by First US Army under Major General Courtney Hodges, through northern France and the Low Countries and into Germany. Montgomery's point was that German opposition against him was negligible, but that there was not enough transport to keep all three Army Groups advancing at full stretch over 500km (300 miles) from Normandy. Even the fleets of Allied transport aircraft intended to mount airborne operations were being committed to ferrying supplies to 21st and 12th Army Groups. Montgomery asked Eisenhower to appoint a ground commander to execute the

'single thrust', even offering to serve under Bradley if necessary, as long as the forces to the south gave up their supplies.

Whatever the merits of this argument, it was firmly opposed by Bradley, for whom Montgomery's conduct of the Battle of Normandy had been profoundly suspect, and who was one of several American commanders who believed that they had won Normandy *despite* Montgomery, and not *because* of him. With final victory in sight it was time for American prowess to display itself, and Montgomery and the British were no longer a factor. Montgomery's plan would also have meant halting the American troops that had advanced farthest towards Germany, Third US Army under Lieutenant General George S. Patton Jr, Montgomery's old rival.

On 23 August, Montgomery at last pressured Eisenhower into agreeing that 21st Army Group's thrust into northern France should have priority in supplies (which Montgomery chose to interpret as absolute priority), to free the English Channel ports for Allied supply ships and overrun the launch sites for the V-1 'buzz-bombs' attacking southern England. Bradley's principal mission was to support this thrust with First US Army, sending most of its divisions north of Aachen. Instead, Bradley quietly connived at Patton's continuing southern thrust towards Germany, holding First US Army back and

directing it increasingly south, away from 21st Army Group. At the end of August, as Third US Army's drive began to halt at the gates of Germany from lack of fuel, relations between Montgomery and the American generals could hardly have been worse.

Allied victory in the Battle of Normandy had also depended very heavily on massive air support for the ground troops, a duty imposed for Eisenhower on the often reluctant airmen by Allied Expeditionary Air Forces (AEAF) under the unpopular Air Chief Marshal Sir Trafford Leigh-Mallory. On 15 August, Leigh-Mallory, also believing that the war in Europe was won, started to close down AEAF Headquarters and plan for his next posting. The Allied heavy bomber forces of RAF Bomber Command and USAAF 8th Air Force went back to their preferred strategy of bombing German cities, while the SHAEF tactical air forces split along national lines, with USAAF 9th Air Force supporting 12th Army Group and RAF 2nd Tactical Air Force supporting 21st Army Group. Since the Luftwaffe (German Air Force) in the west barely existed, and the Allies enjoyed unquestioned air supremacy, this appeared not to matter.

Before D-Day, SHAEF staff had identified the need for a new headquarters to coordinate the various Allied airforces for airborne operations, and as part of the disbanding of the AEAF Eisenhower created Combined Airborne Forces Headquarters on 2 August under Lieutenant General Lewis Brereton, the highly controversial former commander of 9th Air Force, who was disliked by Bradley. On 16 August this name was changed to First Allied Airborne Army as part of the Allied deception plan based around the fictitious First US Army Group (FUSAG), which had fooled the Germans for months.

Under pressure from Washington, where Army Chief of Staff General George C. Marshall and General Henry 'Hap' Arnold, commanding the Army Air Forces, both wanted a major airborne operation mounted in Europe before the end of the war, Eisenhower placed First Allied Airborne Army under 21st Army Group control. As the Allied supply crisis and dispute over strategy worsened, it was from this tangle of conflicting interests that an airborne solution, Operation 'Market-Garden', started to emerge.

THE OPPOSING COMMANDERS

The Allied Commanders

On 1 September, Eisenhower formally took command of the ground battle from Montgomery. Next day, after conferring with Bradley, Hodges and Patton, he issued his own interpretation of priority for Montgomery, a compromise 'two thrust' strategy from north and south including Third US Army's drive in the plan. Communications from SHAEF Headquarters at Granville were very poor, with top priority messages like this taking three days or more to reach Montgomery and Bradley. On the same day Eisenhower was immobilized with a twisted knee, while political demands on his time increased when on 5 September Winston Churchill and the British Chiefs of Staff sailed for Quebec for a major strategy conference with President Roosevelt and his military advisers. In these circumstances, Eisenhower could exercise little control over the land battle or his own quarrelling subordinates.

Montgomery, as was his custom, remained at 21st Army Group Tactical Headquarters, relying on his chief of staff, Major General Francis 'Freddy' de Guingand, to represent him at SHAEF. Unfortunately, on 9 September de Guingand collapsed from exhaustion, and Montgomery sent him home to rest for a week. Montgomery regarded the 'two thrust' strategy as nothing more than the original broad front advance – which could not be sustained. Despite several meetings between Bradley and Montgomery, physical separation and communications problems compounded this breakdown in relations between 21st Army Group and the Americans.

With the activation of SHAEF, Montgomery was promoted from a general commanding all 43 SHAEF divisions to a field marshal commanding

◀ *Lieutenant General Brian Horrocks, taken in Normandy in July 1944, a few days before his collapse. Horrocks had been injured by German aircraft fire while commanding XIII Corps in Italy in June 1943, and never properly recovered. Note the very clear 'Running Boar' formation sign of XXX Corps on his shoulder. (IWM photograph B9532)*

▶ *A Cromwell tank of 1st (Armoured) Battalion of the Coldstream Guards, the Guards Armoured Division, receiving a rapturous welcome in the centre of Brussels on 4 September. The leading troops of the division reached Brussels as darkness fell on the previous day. The rapid advance of XXX Corps from the Seine came as a complete surprise to Montgomery's critics, who thought of him as a slow-moving commander, and transformed the argument for the 'single thrust' strategy. (IWM photograph BU480)*

the fourteen divisions of his own 21st Army Group: in practice, with First Canadian Army occupied clearing the Channel ports, this meant the three Army Corps (eight divisions and four armoured brigades) of Second British Army under Lieutenant General Sir Miles 'Bimbo' Dempsey. As the effective ground commander for 'Market-Garden', Dempsey remains a complete enigma, entirely under the shadow of his illustrious and autocratic superior, for whose mistakes he seemed happy to shoulder the blame.

In Normandy, Montgomery had relied for his major offensives on the talented commander of British VIII Corps, Lieutenant General Sir Richard O'Connor. However, at the start of August, Montgomery brought out an old protégé, Lieutenant General Brian Horrocks ('Jorrocks' to everyone) who was still recovering from wounds, to command British XXX Corps. On 20 August, Horrocks' health collapsed, and he fell ill with fever. Montgomery concealed this fact while Horrocks recovered, and on 26 August he placed XXX Corps at the head of Second British Army's victorious

advance north from the Seine. Horrocks commanded from a tank for the next two weeks as XXX Corps drove forward almost unopposed for 300km (200 miles), liberating Arras on 1 September, Brussels on 3 September, and Antwerp on 4 September, followed by British XII Corps under Lieutenant General Neil Ritchie. Unable to sustain all of Second British Army at this speed, Montgomery ordered VIII Corps to give up its transport and halt on the Seine, where the pragmatic O'Connor began to organize another posting for himself.

At Antwerp, XXX Corps halted, largely from exhaustion and lack of fuel. Although its sudden advance had trapped most of German Fifteenth Army under General Gustav von Zangen between the coast and the River Scheldt (Schelde) estuary, Horrocks failed to advance the short distance north of Antwerp to complete the trap. Instead, after a two-day pause, XXX Corps began to spread out eastward, trying to force the Albert and Meuse-Escaut Canals and press into Holland. On 8 September the first launch of German V-2 rockets

Frederick Arthur Montague Browning, shown with (left) Major General Stanislav Sosabowski, commanding 1st Polish Parachute Brigade which came under his command. Aged 47 in 1944 and a former Grenadier Guards officer, Browning had won the Distinguished Service Order in the First World War, and had first met Churchill when they shared a dugout together in 1916.

against southern England from sites in northern Holland gave extra impetus to the need for Second British Army's advance.

Meanwhile, Lieutenant General Brereton was at SHAEF Headquarters seeking a role for First Allied Airborne Army. A hard-living, hard-drinking former First World War pilot with a remarkable ability to prosper from defeat, Brereton saw his role entirely as an organizer of air power, rather than as an Army commander. He was determined to fulfill General Arnold's wishes by using all three airborne divisions assigned to First Allied Airborne Army in one operation.

Brereton's Deputy Commander for First Allied Airborne Army was also the commander of British I Airborne Corps, Lieutenant General F. A. M. 'Boy' Browning. A dashing figure, he had been appointed by Churchill to command British Airborne Forces in 1941 and had built them up by political and administrative manipulation of the British military establishment as a protégé of Admiral Lord Louis Mountbatten. Disliked and distrusted by the Americans as a 'supercilious English aristocrat', Browning was anxious to lead the troops he had created into battle before the war ended.

Repeatedly during August, airborne operations had been planned and then cancelled as the speed of the Allied advance made them unnecessary. On 2

September a drop by all three divisions near Lille and Courtrai, for which Second British Army halted its own advance, was cancelled at the last moment when Bradley diverted First US Army to liberate the area instead. Matters came to a head next day when Brereton agreed with SHAEF on a new drop to be mounted on 4 September, only to discover that Browning had agreed an entirely different operation with 21st Army Group, using only I Airborne Corps to support an advance northward into Holland by XXX Corps on 6 September. Browning threatened to resign to stop Brereton's plan, leaving relations between the two men very poor. From Eisenhower to Browning and Horrocks, the Allied command chain for 'Market-Garden' was in disarray.

The German Commanders

Since 1941, Adolf Hitler had exercised direct control over German military operations from Oberkommando der Wehrmacht (OKW) Head-quarters at Rastenburg in eastern Germany. On 14 July 1944, a bomb plot to kill Hitler at Rastenburg by German Army officers had only narrowly failed, and senior German officers fought the rest of the war under a cloud of suspicion in which retreat or failure could bring arrest for treason.

▶ *Generalfeldmarschall Gerd von Rundstedt (on the far left) with (gesturing) Obergruppen-führer Josef 'Sepp' Dietrich, briefly commander of Fifth Panzer Army. Von Rundstedt commanded Army Group B from 10 March 1942 until 2 July 1944, being dismissed for insubordination after his criticism of Hitler's conduct of the Battle of Normandy. He nevertheless presided over the German Army 'Court of Honour' following the assassination attempt against Hitler, and felt unable to decline Hitler's recall to active service again in September.*

▶ *Generalfeldmarschall Otto Moritz Walther Model. Aged 53 in 1944, Model had won the Iron Cross First Class and Knight's Cross with Swords in the First World War. Despite his humble origins, he always tried to* *appear as a Prussian aristocrat, even down to his habitual monocle. True to his own view of German military tradition, in April 1945 Model committed suicide rather than face surrender. (IWM photograph MH12850)*

The shock of Second British Army's advance brought an immediate change in the German command in the west. On 3 September, General-feldmarschall Gerd von Rundstedt, an elderly aristocrat whose loyalty was unquestionable, was recalled to take over OB West from General-feldmarschall Model, largely as an administrator, freeing Model to concentrate on Army Group B and the defence of Holland and north-west Germany. Model, a Prussian of non-aristocratic background, had earned his reputation on the Eastern Front as 'the Führer's fireman', able to take charge of a rout and turn it into a counter-attack, which was precisely the challenge he now faced. He at once signalled Rastenburg that he needed a further 25 divisions to stop the Allied drive. Next day, while Model organized the escape of Fifteenth Army across the Scheldt estuary, OKW alerted

General Kurt Student, former commander of the German airborne forces and the leading expert on their use, to take command of a new First Parachute Army under Army Group B, to be formed east of Fifteenth Army with its head-quarters at 's Hertogenbosch in central Holland. Model also ordered II SS Panzer Corps of two armoured divisions, which had been virtually destroyed in the Falaise fighting, to rally close to his own headquarters at Arnhem. The commander of II SS Panzer Corps, Obergruppenführer Wilhelm 'Willi' Bittrich, like Brereton a former pilot and a specialist in defence against airborne operations, had taken command of the Corps on 28 July and led it through the Falaise rout.

▶ *Kurt Student, shown after his promotion to Generaloberst and command of Army Group H following 'Market-Garden'. Born in 1890 of minor Prussian nobility, Student pioneered the use of German airborne forces and commanded them in France in 1940 and in the capture of Crete in 1941, the only completely successful strategic airborne operation of the war. Partly because of the high cost in casualties, the Germans mounted no further major airborne operations after Crete, and Student's career languished until September 1944. (IWM photograph MH6100)*

▶ *Left to right, Major General Allan Adair commanding the Guards Armoured Division, Montgomery, Horrocks, and Major General G. P. B. 'Pip' Roberts commanding 11th Armoured Division, which was transferred from XXX Corps to VIII Corps for 'Market-Garden', taken near the Albert Canal on Friday 15 September. Although Montgomery went to great lengths after 'Market-Garden' to distance himself from the battle, the photographic record suggests that he was heavily involved down to divisional level. Both Horrocks and Montgomery are wearing a type of sleeveless leather jerkin popular with senior British officers, the latter with an RAF flying jacket. (IWM photograph B9973)*

THE OPPOSING ARMIES

The Allied Forces

By September 1944, Second British Army had overcome most of the amateurism that marked British forces earlier in the war and was a victorious army at the height of its abilities. Even so, and although its artillery and engineers were excellent and its infantry almost unbreakable in defence, it had a reputation for slowness and poor coordination when attacking. Having borne the brunt of the heavy fighting in Normandy followed by the pursuit across France, it was also exhausted, with battle fatigue casualties running at epidemic proportions. It was badly short of troops, and to keep it up to strength Montgomery was forced to break up one

division in early September. Those troops that were left, believing the war was virtually won, were increasingly reluctant to risk their lives in battle.

Second British Army had also outrun its own supplies, its tactical Intelligence, and most of its air support. Almost half of 2nd Tactical Air Force was tied up with First Canadian Army, and the rest was searching for suitable airfields in Belgium. As German resistance stiffened, Lieutenant General Dempsey became deeply concerned at the weakness of the proposed northern thrust into Holland, and Montgomery agreed to a delay until 10 September. On that day, the Guards Armoured Division under Major General Allan Adair captured an intact bridge, promptly named 'Joe's Bridge', over the

▲ *The C-47 Dakota (officially named the 'Skytrain' by the USAAF), the workhorse Allied transport aircraft of the war. This particular aircraft is in USAAF IX Troop Carrier Command service for 'Market-Garden' in September 1944. The markings on its fuselage show that it has made three paratroop drops,* *five casualty evacuation flights, and fourteen cargo flights (the 'camel' symbol). The commandeering of their aircraft for supply flights in this way was a constant source of trouble for the airborne forces. With the paratroops (probably Poles) in front of the Dakota is one of its crew, in flying jacket and baseball cap.*

Meuse-Escaut Canal (50ms wide) near Neerpelt, and became the natural choice to lead the advance of XXX Corps under the still sickly Horrocks.

Like other British armoured divisions, the Guards Armoured had abandoned its formal organization in Normandy, adopting a 'group' structure that paired an armoured battalion with a trucked battalion of the same regiment. Guardsmen were specially selected, and the division had a high reputation; but, as with other British divisions, the infantry shortage had forced it to reduce some battalions from three to two companies, and many of its recent replacements had come from other formations such as anti-aircraft artillery batteries. In all, the Guards Armoured Division probably numbered about 13,000 men and 200 tanks. After taking 1,400 casualties during two months in Normandy, it had lost a further 600 men in ten days' fighting along the Belgian canals, leaving it with few illusions about German fighting intentions.

Exact figures for higher formations have little meaning, but XXX Corps numbered at least 100,000 troops, and Second British Army more than 800,000 in total.

Also on 10 September, the still-crippled Eisenhower flew out to Brussels with his deputy, Air Chief Marshal Sir Arthur Tedder, to meet Montgomery at last. This highly charged meeting produced another change of plan. In return for the promise of more supplies from Eisenhower, Montgomery would delay his drive northwards into Holland in order to use the whole of Second British Army and First Allied Airborne Army together. The plan was codenamed 'Market-Garden', and if it

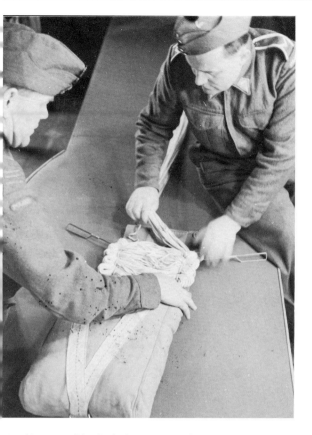

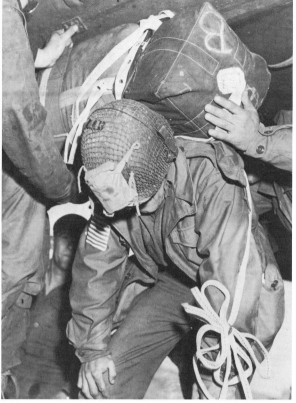

▲ *Aircrew of 1st Polish Parachute Brigade, which used British equipment, packing a parachute. Made of silk, nylon or a type of cotton, the British 'X-Type' parachute was meant to be virtually foolproof, and no reserve parachute was carried (American paratroops carried two T-5 type parachutes).*

▲ *An American paratrooper helps shoulder an equipment-carrying 'parapack' into position on board his aircraft. The man is wearing the new M1943 uniform with a US flag 'invasion patch' but no divisional patch on his other sleeve, suggesting a training exercise just before 'Market-Garden'. The wearing of a first aid pack or field dressing on the front of the helmet was common practice.*

succeeded Montgomery hoped to use it to force Eisenhower into accepting the 'single thrust' north.

During September, Lieutenant General Brereton increased First Allied Airborne Army's staff from 323 officers and men to 1,385. Its air component was about 1,300 C-47 Dakota aircraft, and 250 Albemarles, Halifaxes and Stirlings of the RAF, together with about 2,000 gliders. Transport pilots were regarded as non-combatants by the USAAF and generally ranked well below fighter and bomber crews. Unlike the Americans, British glider pilots and pathfinders were trained to fight as infantry in their own units once on the ground.

The ground element of First Allied Airborne Army was about 35,000 combat troops who would fly into action, plus a 'seaborne tail' to follow later.

US XVIII Airborne Corps Headquarters under Lieutenant General Matthew Ridgway was complete by September, but Lieutenant General Browning was still busy turning his British Airborne Forces administrative headquarters into British I Airborne Corps Headquarters. In particular, Browning's signals section was only created on 2 September, and he had no direct liaison with 2nd Tactical Air Force or other Allied airforces. Attempts very late in the planning of Operation 'Market-Garden' to provide air liaison officers resulted in failure. Like Horrocks at XXX Corps, Browning also had no Dutch liaison officer at his headquarters; however, all the airborne divisions

had Dutch liaison officers for 'Market-Garden'.

The 82nd US Airborne Division and 101st US Airborne Division each had three regiments (each three battalions strong) of parachute infantry, who were all volunteers, and one of airlanding infantry in gliders, who were not. Each division had 36 field guns, twice as many as a British airborne division. All these troops were specially trained and of the highest quality, and both they and their commanders had recent battle experience. The two divisions were busy absorbing more than 10,000 replacements for casualties suffered in Normandy.

◀ *A Sergeant Pilot of the Glider Pilot Regiment, wearing his rank badges and pilot's wings (with an enclosed letter 'G' identifying him as a Second Pilot) on the Denison smock, and armed with a Mark IV Short Magazine Lee-Enfield rifle. The other man, carrying the standard Bren light machine-gun, may belong to any of the British Airborne units at Arnhem as unit and rank badges (except for NCOs) were not normally worn on the smock. He wears an early-pattern helmet with black leather straps, and has tied his face veil as a cape over his shoulders.*

▶ *British paratroop kit being explained to King George VI at an inspection in May 1944. On display is the British version of the 'leg bag' carrying the soldier's equipment. This was released during descent to dangle beneath the paratrooper on a restraining rope to minimize the danger of injury on landing. This bag holds a PIAT (Projector Infantry Anti-Tank), with an effective range of about 50m. (IWM photograph H36712)*

ALLIED ORDER OF BATTLE

SUPREME HEADQUARTERS ALLIED EXPEDITIONARY FORCES (SHAEF)
Supreme Commander: General Dwight D. Eisenhower
Deputy Supreme Commander: Air Chief Marshal Sir Arthur Tedder
Chief of Staff: Major General Walter Bedell Smith

12th ARMY GROUP

Lieutenant General Omar N. Bradley

FIRST US ARMY (from 24 September)
Lieutenant General Courtney H. Hodges

XIX US CORPS
Major General Charles H. Corlett

2nd Armored Division
30th Infantry Division
7th Armored Division (from 27 September)
29th Infantry Division (from 27 September)
113th Cavalry Group

21st ARMY GROUP

Field Marshal Sir Bernard Montgomery
Chief of Staff: Major General F. W. de Guingand

SECOND BRITISH ARMY
Lieutenant General Sir Miles Dempsey

XII CORPS
Lieutenant General N. M. Ritchie

7th Armoured Division
Major General G. L. Verney

15th (Scottish) Division
Major General C. M. Barber

53rd (Welsh) Division
Major General R. K. Ross

VIII CORPS
Lieutenant General Sir Richard O'Connor

11th Armoured Division
Major General G. P. B. Roberts

3rd Division
Major General L. G. Whistler

4th Armoured Brigade
Brigadier R. M. P. Carver

1st Belgian Brigade
Colonel B. Piron

XXX CORPS
Lieutenant General B. G. Horrocks

2nd Household Cavalry Regiment

Guards Armoured Division
Major General A. H. S. Adair
5th Guards Brigade (Grenadiers/Irish)
32nd Guards Brigade (Coldstream/Welsh)

43rd (Wessex) Division
Major General G. I. Thomas
129th Brigade: 4 SLI, 4, 5 Wilts
130th Brigade: 7 Hamps, 4, 5 Dorsets
214th Brigade: 7 SLI, 1 Worcs, 5 DCLI
Machine Gun Battalion: 8 Middlesex

50th (Northumbrian) Division (to VIII Corps
18 September)
Major General D. A. H. Graham
69th Brigade: 5 East Yorks, 6, 7 Green Howards
151th Brigade: 6, 8, 9 DLI
231st Brigade: 2 Devons, 1 Hamps, 1 Dorsets
Machine Gun Battalion: 2 Cheshires

8th Armoured Brigade
Brigadier E. G. Prior-Palmer

Royal Netherlands Brigade 'Prinses Irene'
Colonel A. de Ruyter van Steveninck

FIRST ALLIED AIRBORNE ARMY
Lieutenant General Lewis H. Brereton
Deputy: Lieutenant General F. A. M. Browning

AIR ELEMENT

USAAF IX TROOP CARRIER COMMAND
Major General Paul L. Williams
52 Wing: 61, 313, 314, 315, 316, 349 Groups (Dakota)
53 Wing: 434, 435, 436, 437, 438 Groups (Dakota)
50 Wing: 439, 440, 441, 442 Groups (Dakota)
Total: 60 Squadrons 1,100 aircraft

RAF 38 GROUP
Air Vice Marshal L. N. Hollinghurst
190, 196, 295, 299, 570, 620 Sq (Stirling)
296, 287, 298, 644 Sq (Halifax/Albemarle)
Total: 12 Squadrons 240 aircraft

RAF 46 GROUP
Air Commodore A. L. Fiddament (to 15 Sept)/
Air Commodore L. Darvall
48, 233, 271, 437 (RCAF), 512, 575 Sqn (Dakota)
Total: 6 Squadrons, 279 aircraft

GROUND ELEMENT:

XVIII US AIRBORNE CORPS (HQ secondary role only in battle)
Major General Matthew B. Ridgway

82nd ('All American') Airborne Division
Brigadier General James Gavin
504th Parachute Infantry Regiment
505th Parachute Infantry Regiment
508th Parachute Infantry Regiment
325th Glider Infantry Regiment
376th Parachute Field Artillery Battalion
319th Glider Field Artillery Battalion
320th Glider Field Artillery Battalion

101st ('Screaming Eagles') Airborne Division
Major General Maxwell Taylor
501st Parachute Infantry Regiment
502nd Parachute Infantry Regiment
506th Parachute Infantry Regiment
327th Glider Infantry Regiment
377th Parachute Field Artillery Battalion
321st Glider Field Artillery Battalion
907th Glider Field Artillery Battalion

I BRITISH AIRBORNE CORPS
Lieutenant General F. A. M. Browning

1st Airborne Division
Major General R. E. Urquhart
1st Parachute Brigade: 1, 2, 3 Para
4th Parachute Brigade: 10, 11, 156 Para
1st Airlanding Brigade: 1 Border, 2 South Staffs,
7 KOSBs
1st Airlanding Light Regiment, Royal Artillery

1st Polish Independent Parachute Brigade
Major General Stanislav Sosabowski
1, 2, 3 Parachute Infantry.

52nd (Lowland) Division (airportable)
Major General E. Hakewell-Smith
155th Brigade: 7/9 Royal Scots, 4 KOSB, 6 HLI
156th Brigade: 4/5 R Scots Fusiliers,
6 Cameronians, 1 Glasgow Highlanders
157th Brigade: 5 KOSB, 7 Cameronians, 5 HLI
Machine Gun Battalion: 7 Manchesters
79, 80, 186 Field Regiments, 1 Mountain
Regiment, 54 Anti-Tank Regiment Royal Artillery

AIR FORCES

RAF SECOND TACTICAL AIR FORCE
Air Marshal Sir Arthur Coningham

RAF 83 GROUP
Air Vice Marshal H. Broadhurst
39 (RCAF) Reconnaissance Wing (Spitfire)
121, 122, 123, 143 Wings (Typhoon)
125, 126 (RCAF), 127 (RCAF) Wings (Spitfire)
Total: 29 Squadrons, 350 aircraft

RAF 2 GROUP
Air Vice Marshal B. E. Embry
136, 138, 140 Wings (Mosquito)
137, 139 Wings (B-25 Mitchell)
Total: 13 Squadrons, 160 aircraft

RAF 84 GROUP (not involved in the battle)
Air Vice Marshal E. O. Brown

AIR FORCES INVOLVED ON 17 SEPTEMBER:

RAF AIR DEFENCE OF GREAT BRITAIN (FIGHTER COMMAND)
Air Marshal Sir Roderic Hill

RAF BOMBER COMMAND
Air Chief Marshal Sir Arthur Harris

RAF COASTAL COMMAND
Air Chief Marshal Sir Sholto Douglas

USAAF 9TH AIR FORCE
Lieutenant General Hoyt S. Vandenberg

USAAF 8TH AIR FORCE
Lieutenant General James H. Doolittle

A Sergeant (1st Class) of 2nd (Dutch) Troop, 10th (Inter-Allied) Commando, members of which were dropped with the British at Arnhem. He also wears British battledress and equipment (note the rubber boots) including a British Commando's green beret with a black-backed 'Lion' badge, and the sleeve badge of British Combined Operations above the Dutch national badge. His shoulder titles are '10 Commando' on the left side, and 'Commando' on the right.

1st British Airborne Division consisted of two brigades of the Parachute Regiment, all volunteers from other units, and an airlanding brigade of infantry battalions, plus the attached 1st Polish Parachute Brigade under Major General Stanislav Sosabowski. Many of its battalions had considerable previous combat experience and, like the Americans, its troops were of the highest quality. But it had never fought before as a division, nor under its current commander, Major General R. E. 'Roy' Urquhart. Waiting in reserve was 52nd (Lowland) Division, a British infantry division organized to be airportable in C-47 Dakotas once airfields were provided for it, together with two small specialist airfield engineer units, one British and one American.

The German Forces

On 1 September OB West reported that it possessed the equivalent of nine infantry divisions and two weak armoured divisions north of the Ardennes, and was outnumbered ten to one in tanks, three to one in artillery, and absolutely in aircraft. The capture of Antwerp on 4 September provoked 'Mad Tuesday' next day, as German rear-area troops of Armed Forces Command Netherlands fell back in chaos throughout Holland. In these circumstances, any accurate count of German forces opposing 'Market-Garden' was impossible, but Allied estimates suggest no more than 15,000 troops and 250 tanks by 7 September. Model's great achievement was his organization of a coherent defence in just ten more days from this. Altogether 82,000 men, 46,000 vehicles and 530 guns of Fifteenth Army escaped across the Scheldt estuary by 23 September, and some were able to reinforce First Parachute Army by the time 'Market-Garden' started. Other troops came virtually untrained from reserve units, or were grouped together in improvised formations.

The basic German fighting unit for 'Market-Garden' was the Kampfgruppe (battle-group), an improvised formation of no fixed size or strength. Some were smaller than battalions, but those that played an important role in 'Market-Garden' are best regarded as wrecked and reconstituted divisions, very weak in infantry but

GERMAN ORDER OF BATTLE

The German order of battle for 'Market-Garden' changed daily. These are the main formations involved .

REICHSFUHRER HAUPTQUARTIER (RFH)/ OBERKOMMANDO DER WEHRMACHT (OKW)
Commander in Chief: Adolf Hitler
Chief of Staff: Generalfeldmarschall Wilhelm Keitel   Chief of Operations: Generaloberst Alfred Jodel

OBERBEFELSHABER WEST (OB WEST)
Generalfeldmarschall Gerd von Rundstedt

ARMED FORCES COMMAND (AFC) NETHERLANDS

General der Flieger Friedrich Christiansen

II SS PANZER CORPS (to Army Group B 17 September)
Obergruppenführer Wilhelm Bittrich

SS-Kampfgruppe 'Hohenstauffen'
Obersturmbahnführer Walther Harzer

SS-Kampfgruppe 'Frundsberg'
Brigadeführer Heinz Harmel

'Hermann Goering' Division Training Regiment
Oberstleutnant Fritz Fullreide

Kampfgruppe 'Von Tettau'
Generalleutnant Hans von Tettau

ARMY GROUP B

Generalfeldmarschall Walther Model

FIFTEENTH ARMY
General der Infanterie Gustav von Zangen

LXVII CORPS
General der Infanterie Otto Sponheimer

346th Infantry Division
Generalleutnant Erich Diester

711th Static Division
Generalleutnant Josef Reichert

719th Coastal Division
Generalleutnant Karl Sievers

LXXXVIII CORPS
General der Infanterie Hans Reinhard

Kampfgruppe 'Chill'
Generalleutnant Kurt Chill

59th Infantry Division
Generalleutnant Walter Poppe

245th Infantry Division
Oberst Gerhard Kegler

712th Static Division
Generalleutnant Friedrich-Wilhelm Neuman

FIRST PARACHUTE ARMY
General der Fallschirmtruppen Kurt Student

LXXXVI CORPS
General der Infanterie Hans von Obstfelder

176th Infantry Division
Oberst Christian Landau

Kampfgruppe 'Walther'

6th Parachute Regiment
Oberstleutnant Friedrich Freiherr von der Heydte

107th Panzer Brigade
Major Freiherr von Maltzahn

Division 'Erdmann'
Generalleutnant Wolfgang Erdmann

II PARACHUTE CORPS (from 19 September)
General der Fallschirmtruppen Eugen Meindl

XII SS CORPS (from 29 September)
Obergruppenführer Kurt von Gottberg

180th Infantry Division
Generalleutnant Bernard Klosterkemper

190th Infantry Division
Generalleutnant Ernst Hammer

363rd Volksgrenadier Division (from 5 October)
Generalleutnant Augustus Dettling

Continued overleaf

GERMAN ORDER OF BATTLE *CONTINUED FROM OVERLEAF*

WEHRKREIS VI

CORPS 'FELDT' (from 18 September)
General der Kavalerie Kurt Feldt

406th Landesschützen Division
Generalleutnant Scherbening

LUFTWAFFE WEST

(directly under **LUFTFLOTTE REICH**)

Approximately 300 Bf 109, Fw 190 and Me 262 fighters,
120 Ju 87 and Ju 88 bombers, very low on fuel.

---

strong in artillery and assault guns, with a size and combat power roughly equal to an Allied brigade. Kampfgruppe 'Walther', defending against XXX Corps, changed its structure daily, including troops from the Army, Navy, Luftwaffe and Waffen-SS, and existed for less than a month (its commander's full identity has not survived). Kampfgruppe 'Chill' was formed by Generalleutnant Kurt Chill from the remains of his own 85th Infantry Division together with 84th and 89th Infantry Divisions. Even ordinary German formations in 'Market-Garden' were rarely at full strength. Generalleutnant Walter Poppe's 59th Infantry Division was barely 1,000 men, 30 guns and eighteen assault guns, while 6th Parachute Regiment was without one of its battalions. Commanding or coordinating attacks between these improvised formations was extremely difficult, and they varied greatly in quality.

After its retreat from the Falaise pocket, II SS Panzer Corps claimed on 12 September to have only twelve functioning tanks. By this date 9th SS Panzer Division had formed itself into SS-Kampfgruppe 'Hohenstauffen' under its senior surviving officer, Obersturmbahnführer Walther Harzer. After sending troops to Kampfgruppe 'Walther', this consisted of a company of PzKpfw IV and PzKpfw V Panther tanks, two batteries of Jagdpanther IV assault guns, a reconnaissance battalion, a weak panzergrenadier regiment, and an artillery

battalion (twelve guns). SS-Kampfgruppe 'Frundsberg', formed from 10th SS Panzer Division under Brigadeführer Heinz Harmel, had only a few PzKpfw IVs and Jagdpanthers, its reconnaissance battalion and panzergrenadier regiment, but two artillery battalions. The total force was probably no more than 3,000 men with a high proportion of heavy infantry weapons and machine-guns. Like the Allied airborne troops, they were of the highest fighting quality.

Exhausted, routed or untrained, the Germans were indeed prepared to fight, although most were perfectly aware that the war was lost. Some, particularly in the Waffen-SS, had little wish to survive to face disgrace and possible war crimes trials. As the Allies pushed closer to German soil, most were ready to defend their homeland against an invader who demanded unconditional surrender, and whose attacks were visibly weakening.

▶ *The bridge over the River Maas (Meuse) at Grave, with nine spans measuring 600m in length across a river 250m wide, was a substantial objective for 82nd Airborne Division. Its ominous name (usually pro-nounced to rhyme with 'Marv') led to some late attempts on the part of American staff officers to call it 'Gravey bridge'. This picture was taken on 27 September at the end of the battle. (IWM photograph B10347)*

THE OPPOSING PLANS

The Allied Plan

Immediately after Montgomery's conference with Eisenhower, Dempsey ordered Browning to start planning I Airborne Corps' part in the battle. One later version of this meeting had Browning telling Montgomery that his troops could hold Arnhem bridge for four days, but that this might prove 'a bridge too far'. There is no evidence for this unlikely story, and planning was based on a general estimate of Second British Army reaching Arnhem in two to five days rather than to a fixed timetable.

Montgomery issued formal orders for Operation 'Market-Garden' on 12 September, after briefing Horrocks. The plan called for First Allied Airborne Army to assist Second British Army in a rapid advance from the Meuse-Escaut Canal all the way to Nunspeet on the Zuider Zee (Ijsselmeer) almost 160km (100 miles) away, before turning east into Germany. The airborne troops would capture bridges over the major rivers and canals at three

towns, each with a population in 1944 of about 90,000: Eindhoven, about 20km (13 miles) from the start line, Nijmegen 85km (53 miles) away, and Arnhem 100km (64 miles) away.

The tree-lined double track road along which XXX Corps was to advance ran through countryside that was almost entirely flat, partly of sandy soil and partly *polder* or drained bogland, broken by orchards, copses, small streams and ditches, all making opposed cross-country movement very difficult for vehicles. North of the line from 's Hertogenbosch to Nijmegen the ground was almost all *polder*, veined with hundreds of small drainage ditches. The drained *polder* between the River Waal north of Nijmegen and the Lower Rhine (or Lek), filled with orchards and laced with waterways, was known locally as the *betuwe* or 'island', with roads running along causeways up to 3m above the surrounding fields. North of the Lower Rhine at Arnhem the soil was sandy heathland, rising away north of the town past Apeldoorn to the Veluwe

Market-Garden, The Plan 17 September 1944

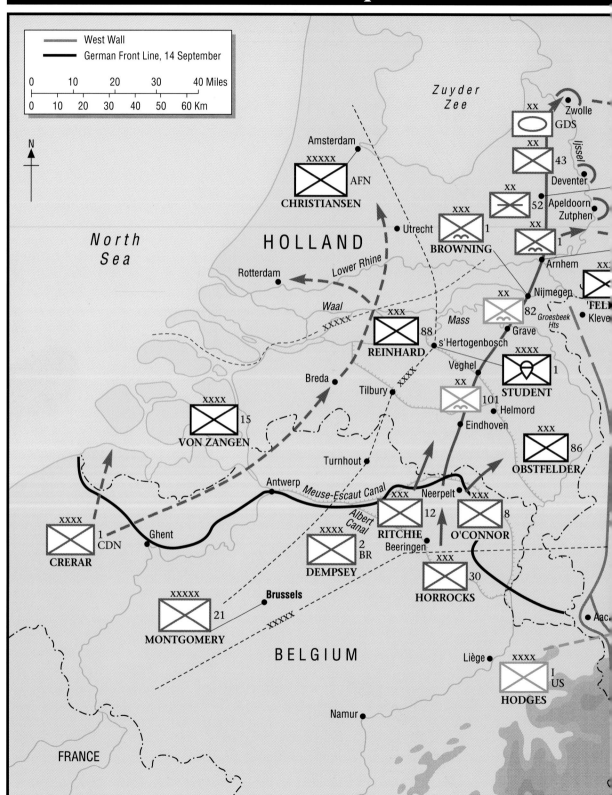

heights, at 100m the highest ground in Holland.

Browning returned to I Airborne Corps Headquarters at Moor Park near London after his meeting with Dempsey, and notified First Allied Airborne Army at Ascot that an air plan was required. Brereton also produced this plan, Operation 'Market', by 12 September. For simplicity, as far as possible all paratroops were to be carried by USAAF aircraft and all gliders towed by RAF aircraft, regardless of the nationality of the troops. Despite predictions of up to 40 per cent aircraft losses, Brereton wanted to prove that a major air assault could be mounted in daylight (there was no moon in the target period, ruling out a night drop), and sided with his pilots by allowing only one major lift each day. As a result, the 'Market' plan would take at least three days to fly the complete airborne divisions to their targets. The fourth day would be spent on resupply, and 52nd (Lowland) Division would be flown in north of Arnhem over the next two days. In order to prevent

◀ *OPERATION 'MARKET', THE AIRBORNE PLAN. On 17 September, First Allied Airborne Army drops three airborne divisions along a corridor north of Eindhoven. 101st US Airborne Division secures bridges from Eindhoven to Veghel. 82nd US Airborne Division secures bridges from Grave to Nijmegen and the Groesbeek heights. 1st British Airborne Division secures Arnhem bridge and the high ground to the north.*

OPERATION 'GARDEN', THE GROUND PLAN. Simultaneous with 'Market' on 17 September, Second British Army drives northwards from the Meuse–Escaut Canal on a very narrow front, led by XXX Corps, which links up with each of the airborne divisions in turn. Flanking attacks by XII Corps and VIII Corps on either side protect this drive. Once north of Arnhem, XXX Corps establishes the Guards Armoured Division on the Zuider Zee with a bridgehead over the River Ijssel at Zwolle, and 43rd Division with a bridgehead at Deventer. Once Apeldoorn is secure, 52nd Division is flown in to reinforce this position and secure a bridgehead at Zutphen.

With four divisions established north of the Lower Rhine, XXX Corps leads Second British Army east towards Osnabruck and/or south-east towards Hamm to encircle the Ruhr, possibly in conjunction with First US Army from the south. Meanwhile, First Canadian Army clears the remainder of the Netherlands and the V-2 sites.

◀ *An aerial view looking west.of the River Waal flowing through the centre of Nijmegen, taken by an RAF reconnaissance aircraft on the evening of 22 September at the height of the battle, The road bridge (bottom of picture) and railway bridge, both about 650m long, can be clearly seen (note the shadows showing the shape of both bridges). Although Browning's plan gave no priority to capture of the railway bridge, Allied engineers could convert such a bridge to take armoured vehicles within a day. (IWM photograph CL1203)*

confusion over the target, Brereton also ruled that while his flights from England were in the air 2nd Tactical Air Force must remain grounded rather than flying into the same airspace. Allied meteorologists predicted at least two days of clear weather starting on Sunday 17 September, which became 'D-Day' for the battle.

Brereton agreed that Browning's I Airborne Corps would command all three divisions of First Allied Airborne Army, with XVIII Airborne Corps relegated to an administrative role. Browning's plan was for each of the first wave to land as a formed body in open country about 10km (6 miles) from its main objective, and then advance to capture it. If everything worked, each of the three complete divisions would finish after three days holding an all-round perimeter of at least 40km (25 miles) while the ground forces arrived.

These distances and timescales only made sense if the German troops were not in fact going to fight. Although handicapped by poor coordination between SHAEF, 21st Army Group and First Allied Airborne Army, the Allied picture of German forces in the 'Market-Garden' area was reasonably clear. Browning's plan estimated the Germans at Arnhem as one broken panzer division, or the equivalent of 3,000 infantry with a few tanks, which was exactly right. Allied Intelligence had tracked II SS Panzer Corps Headquarters back from France to the Eindhoven-Arnhem area before losing it on 4 September, and had identified First Parachute Army Headquarters near 's Hertogenbosch and Army Group B near Arnhem itself by 16 September. The only significant Allied error was a SHAEF belief that II SS Panzer Corps might have retreated to the Kleve area, east of Nijmegen, rather than north.

In Browning's plan, 101st Airborne Division under Major General Maxwell Taylor was to drop north of Eindhoven, to capture the bridges over the River Aa and the larger Willems Canal (30m wide) at Veghel, over the minor River Dommel at St Oedenrode, and over the Wilhelmina Canal (35m wide) at Son, and then go on to capture Eindhoven by nightfall. Originally, Browning had wanted Taylor to secure the road from Eindhoven to Grave, a perimeter of 65km (40 miles). Taylor protested, and Dempsey overruled Browning, allowing 101st

Airborne to halt at Veghel and leave a gap of about 20km (13 miles) in the Allied deployment. Even so, Taylor planned to take all three of his parachute infantry regiments on the first day, believing that artill-ery support would soon arrive from XXX Corps.

Brigadier General James Gavin, Ridgway's successor commanding 82nd Airborne Division, also believed that Browning had set him too large a task, but chose not to protest. Because of the expected threat from the Kleve region, Browning made Gavin's first priority the capture of the Groesbeek heights, an area of wooded hills about 100m high and 12km (8 miles) long to the east of Nijmegen, followed by the bridges over the River Maas (Meuse) at Grave (250m wide) and over the Maas-Waal Canal (60m wide). Only then was 82nd Airborne to try for the road bridge over the Waal (300m wide) in the centre of Nijmegen. Gavin took a mixed force of infantry and artillery on his first lift, realizing that he might have to fight alone for some time.

The landing zones for 1st British Airborne Division under Major General Urquhart were on the heathland west of Arnhem. But Browning specified that Urquhart's main objective was to be the road bridge over the Lower Rhine (100m wide) in the town centre, together with the railway bridge and a nearby pontoon bridge (discovered late on 16 September to have been dismantled by the Germans). Urquhart's troops, joined by 1st Polish Parachute Brigade, would then secure the high ground just north of Arnhem. Urquhart decided to lead with his airlanding troops, and take half his artillery and anti-tank guns on the first lift. Suggestions that a small party of paratroops or glider troops could land directly on Arnhem bridge from the south came too late to change the plan.

On 16 September at Leopoldsburg (Bourg Leopold) about 20km (13 miles) south of Joe's Bridge, Horrocks briefed XXX Corps' senior officers on 'Garden', the ground plan. The Guards Armoured Division would lead XXX Corps' drive northward, codenamed the 'Club Route', aided by flank attacks from XII Corps on the left and VIII Corps (which had just begun to move from the Seine) on the right. As XXX Corps linked up with each airborne division it would take them under command from I Airborne Corps, handing off its troops further south to VIII Corps as it did so.

If the main bridges at Grave, Nijmegen or Arnhem were destroyed, the Guards Armoured would secure the river bank and 43rd (Wessex) Division following would mount an assault crossing. Both divisions were issued rations for four days and fuel for 400km (250 miles). Horrocks' main concern was breaking through the German defenders between Joe's Bridge and Valkenswaard, believed to be six battalions and 20 armoured vehicles. In fact Kampfgruppe 'Walther' had ten weak battalions (including 6th Luftwaffe Penal Battalion in tropical uniforms) and ten assault guns defending the bridghead. Once this German 'crust' was broken, Horrocks expected easy going.

The German Plan

Strictly, there was no German plan for 'Market--Garden'. Some form of Allied advance from the Meuse-Escaut Canal was expected, but German tactical Intelligence was so bad that Kampfgruppe 'Walther' believed that it was facing Canadians, while during the battle SS-Kampfgruppe 'Frundsberg' identified the Guards Armoured Division as Americans.

At the highest level, German defensive plans were based on two assessments of Allied intentions. One threat was an amphibious landing by the (completely fictitious) Fourth British Army on the Dutch coast to cut off the remaining troops of Fifteenth Army. The other was a drive north-east towards Wesel by 21st Army Group as part of a pincer move to encircle the Ruhr. The Germans expected landings by First Allied Airborne Army to support either of these operations, and Generalfeldmarschall Model deployed the meagre forces of Student's First Parachute Army in central Holland to cover them both, exactly in the path of 'Market-Garden'. Model's personal headquarters was the Hartenstein Hotel in Oosterbeek, just east of 1st British Airborne's planned landing sites.

II SS Panzer Corps was not part of Model's defence, coming under Armed Forces Command Netherlands while it rested. Obergruppenführer Bittrich's own headquarters was at Doetinchem, 25km (15 miles) east of Arnhem, with his troops spread out between Arnhem and Deventer. On 12 September SS-Kampfgruppe 'Hohenstauffen' was ordered to start entraining for Siegen near Koblenz in Germany, where it would be refitted. The last of its vehicles were due to leave on 17 September, after which SS-Kampfgruppe 'Frundsberg' was to move to Aachen to refit. On 16 September Bittrich sent Brigadeführer Harmel by car to SS Headquarters in Berlin to plead in person for reinforcements, while Obersturmbahnführer Harzer continued to train his troops. The Allied landings next day would come as a complete surprise.

◀ *British paratroops of 1st Parachute Brigade boarding a C-47 Dakota of USAAF IX Troop Carrier Command on the morning of Sunday 17 September. The soldiers are wearing their parachutes and harness over the sleeveless version of the parachute smock or 'jump jacket' introduced in 1944. Modelled on the German version, this zip-fronted gabardine garment was worn over the Denison smock and discarded on landing. (IWM photograph K7588)*

THE AIR ARMADA, 16 TO 17 SEPTEMBER

What was to become the Battle of Arnhem began an hour before midnight on Saturday 16 September (British Summer Time, equal to GMT plus one hour but an hour behind local time in Holland) as 200 Lancasters and 23 Mosquitos of RAF Bomber Command dropped 890 tons of bombs on four German fighter airfields in northern Holland, including one for Me 262 jet fighters. This was the start of Brereton's plan to deliver the ground troops safely to the target by suppressing the German defences, estimated as including 112 light and 44 heavy anti-aircraft guns. Over the next 24 hours, 1,395 bomber sorties and 1,240 fighter sorties were flown in support of Operation 'Market-Garden'.

The bombing continued at 0800 next day as 822 B-17 Flying Fortresses of 8th Air Force with 161 P-51 Mustangs in escort bombed all 117 identified German anti-aircraft positions along the 'Market-Garden' route, together with airfields at Eindhoven, Deelen and Ede. These were backed up by 54 Lancasters and five Mosquitos of Bomber Command, while another 85 Lancasters and fifteen Mosquitos attacked the anti-aircraft positions on Walcheren island. Two Flying Fortresses, two Lancasters and three Mosquitos were lost. Such was Allied air superiority that these attacks scarcely registered as unusual with the Germans. To coincide with Operation 'Market-Garden', the Dutch Government in exile in London called for a general strike of transport workers throughout the Netherlands.

Sunday 17 September, D-Day for 'Market-Garden', dawned as a beautiful late summer day, slightly cloudy with good visibility. In England, the airborne troops started to board their aircraft. The slower glider tugs, which cruised at 120mph, took off first at 0930, followed by the C-47 Dakota paratroop carrier aircraft at 140mph. The pathfinders, who would arrive first, took off at 1025. Crossing north-east of London, the sky train

A Sergeant Glider Pilot (identified as a First Pilot by the crown at the centre of his pilot's winged badge) wearing MRC body armour, developed by the British Medical Research Council in 1941. Arnhem was probably the only occasion on which MRC armour was worn in action. In theory, MRC armour was worn under the battledress, but the method shown was more comfortable.

◄ *Lieutenant General Browning poses for a photograph with Air Chief Marshal Tedder and an American brigadier general on the morning of Sunday 17 September, a few hours before Browning's glider took off. Although the senior Allied airman in the European theatre, Tedder like Montgomery distanced himself from 'Market-Garden' after its failure. (IWM photograph CH13856)*

▶ *Top: The pathfinders of 1st British Airborne Division's 21st Independent Parachute Company waiting to take off from RAF Fairford on the morning of Sunday 17 September. Behind them are their transport aircraft, Short Stirlings of 620 Squadron, RAF 38 Group. Employed to mark the landing sites with lights, panels and radar homing beacons for the approaching aircraft, pathfinders were regarded as an élite. Unlike their American equivalent, who were drawn from their own parent units, the men of 21st Independent Parachute Company*

resolved itself into two streams, with 101st Airborne Division on the southern route into Holland, and both 82nd Airborne Division and 1st British Airborne Division on the northern route. I Airborne Corps Headquarters took off in gliders behind 82nd Airborne, including Browning's personal chef and wine cellar.

Before boarding his own Horsa glider, Urquhart told his chief staff officer, Lieutenant Colonel Charles Mackenzie, that in the unlikely event of both himself and Brigadier Gerald Lathbury, commanding 1st Parachute Brigade and 1st British

Airborne's senior brigadier, being killed or captured command of the division should pass to Brigadier P. H. W. 'Pip' Hicks, commanding 1st Airlanding Brigade and flying in that day, rather than to Brigadier J. W. 'Shan' Hackett of 4th Parachute Brigade, who was senior to Hicks but not due to arrive until 18 September. Urquhart preferred the elderly and solid Hicks to Hackett, a 33-year-old cavalryman with a background in special forces.

By 1135 the last aircraft had left the ground. The two columns of the sky train each stretched for 150km (94 miles) in length and 5km (three miles) in

trained and fought as a unit. *(IWM photograph CL1154)*

▼ *Below: Fully laden paratroopers of 101st Airborne Division board their C-47 Dakota on the morning of Sunday 17 September. The jump goggles of the soldier far left were not standard issue, and many paratroopers carried non-regulation or semi-regulation items of equipment into battle. The tape or ties below the knees of the uniform trousers were standard practice.*

breadth. On the southern route, 101st Airborne was carried by 424 Dakotas and 70 glider/tug combinations. On the northern route, 82nd Airborne travelled in 482 Dakotas and 50 glider/tug combinations, followed by the 38 glider/tugs (enough for an infantry battalion) of I Airborne Corps Headquarters. 1st British Airborne led as planned with 1st Airlanding Brigade and its artillery and divisional troops in 358 glider/tugs, with 1st Parachute Brigade following in 145 Dakotas. The total was 1,051 troop carrier aircraft and 516 glider/tug combinations, or 2,083 aircraft in all, flying at an average height of 1,500ft (500m). Escort

on the northern route came from 371 Spitfires, Tempests and Mosquitos of Fighter Command, with 548 P-47 Thunderbolts, P-38 Lightnings and P-51 Mustangs of 8th Air Force on the southern route. Average flight time was between 90 and 150 minutes to target.

At about 1200 local time, all 117 German anti-aircraft positions along the 'Market-Garden' route were bombed and strafed once again by 212 Thunderbolts of 9th Air Force, while 50 Mosquitos, 48 Mitchells and 24 Bostons (the RAF version of the A-20 Havoc) of RAF 2 Group bombed German barracks and airfields at Nijmegen, Deelen, Ede and

Operation Market: The Allied Fly-in, 17 September 19

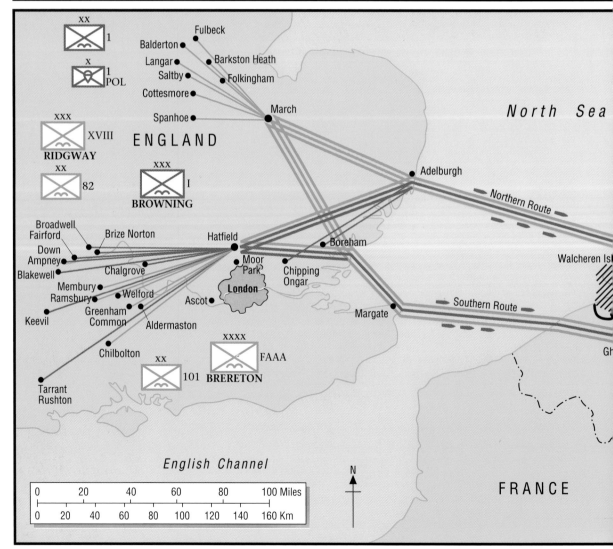

Kleve. Allied pilots reported German anti-aircraft crews abandoning their positions before the aircraft attacked. At 1240, twelve RAF Stirlings dropped the British pathfinders of 21st Independent Parachute Company to the west of Arnhem. At the same time, four USAAF Dakotas released the pathfinders of 101st Airborne north of Eindhoven, and two more put the pathfinders of 82nd Airborne down near Grave bridge. The main drop of 82nd Airborne on to the Groesbeek heights would go in without pathfinders to achieve surprise, directly on top of the anti-aircraft batteries.

Meanwhile, the two great columns of transport

▲ *Lieutenant General Browning designed his own uniform as commander of British Airborne Forces and wore it into action for 'Market-Garden'. Made of barathea, it had a false Uhlan-style front and a zip opening at the neck, displaying a regulation shirt and tie, and was worn with medal ribbons, collar patches and rank badges on the shoulders.*

The highly polished brown 'Sam Browne' belt and swagger stick are correct for a Guards officer. For 'Market-Garden' Browning also wore grey kid gloves. The only indication that he is in Airborne Forces is the famous red beret (which he introduced), with the cap badge correct for his rank. (IWM photograph H21248)

—— German Front Line
//// Heavy German Flak
— Rescue Boats

aircraft had crossed into enemy airspace. The Dakotas, without armour, guns or self-sealing fuel tanks, slowed to 110mph and decended to 500ft (160m) for the drop. The average time over the German anti-aircraft positions was about 40 minutes. On the southern route, Brereton and Ridgway each watched from a Flying Fortress with the 101st Airborne. Of 75 German fighters scrambled, about 30 reached the sky train, but were seen off by its escort. The only dogfight was over Wesel, where seven out of fifteen Me 109s were lost for one American fighter. The anti-aircraft defences were least damaged over Eindhoven, where 101st Airborne lost 33 Dakotas and Brereton's own aircraft was holed. Some gliders failed to complete the trip, or broke up in mid-air. In total 68 Allied aircraft and 71 gliders were lost from all causes in

▲ *British paratroops of 1st Parachute Brigade inside a C-47 Dakota, either about to take off or in flight, on Sunday 17 September. This picture gives some idea of the amount of equipment carried into battle by the paratroops. In addition to*

ALLIED AIR TRANSPORT

AIRCRAFT	Cruising/ towing speed (mph)	Range (miles)	Payload Troops	Payload Supplies/ Equipment (lb)
British				
ALBEMARLE	120	1,350	10	4,000
HALIFAX	130	3,000	10	6,000
STIRLING	120	3,000	12*	6,000
American				
C-47 SKYTRAIN (British name DAKOTA)	140	1,500	20*	6,000

All these aircraft, normally unarmed, were capable of towing one glider at maximum range, or two at shorter ranges, or of carrying the payload shown. A 6,000lb supply load is the equivalent of two large pieces of equipment, e.g., a jeep, trailer or small artillery piece.

*For parachute drops only. For air transport the C-47 could carry up to 28 troops, and the Stirling up to 40 troops.

GLIDERS	Max towing speed (mph)	Stalling speed (mph)	Payload Troops	Payload Equipment/ Supplies (lb)
British				
HORSA	160	60	28	6.900
HAMILCAR*	150	65	–	17,000
American				
CG-4A WACO (British name HADRIAN)	125	38	15	3,750

*The Hamilcar could only be towed by four-engined aircraft such as the Halifax and Stirling. It was designed as a large cargo carrier only, and carried larger calibre artillery pieces or bulldozers. All the gliders had a crew of two pilots.

the flight, including two RAF and eighteen USAAF fighters.

At 1300 the first gliders of 1st Airlanding Brigade skidded to earth west of Arnhem, followed by Urquhart's artillery and divisional troops. Of 319 gliders, 35 failed to arrive, of which 21 landed in England and flew in to Holland next day. The only serious loss was two gliders each carrying a 17pdr anti-tank gun. Meanwhile, Major General Taylor jumped with 6,769 men of 101st Airborne north of Eindhoven. 501st Parachute Infantry Regiment landed correctly on its drop zone south of Veghel, except for 1/501st which was dropped by a fortunate error at Heeswijk, 5km (three miles) to the north-west on the wrong side of the Willems Canal and the River Aa. 502nd Parachute Infantry and 506th Parachute Infantry landed together with 101st

their leg bags, two of the men have special weapons cases, probably to protect machine-guns. Note the quick-release ring at the centre of the parachute harness on each man's chest. (IWM photograph K7586)

ALLIED AIRLIFT REQUIREMENTS

Formation	C-47 Dakotas (carrier)	Gliders/Tugs (all kinds)
Parachute battalion (British/American/Polish)	35	-
Parachute brigade/regiment (British/American/Polish)	120-140	20-40
Airlanding battalion	-	60-70
Divisional artillery* (British)	-	160
Field artillery battalion* (American)	-	95
Parachute artillery battalion* (American)	60	
Airborne division	400	700
Airportable division	2,000 (transport only)	

These are approximate figures only.

*A British light artillery regiment and anti-tank regiment was twelve 75mm guns, six 105mm guns, twelve 6pdr A/T guns, and six 17pdr A/T guns. An American field artillery battalion was twelve 75mm guns or parachute artillery battalion.

Airborne Headquarters just north of the Sonsche forest. At the same time, 6,527 men of 82nd Airborne dropped successfully for the loss of two Dakotas south of Nijmegen, Brigadier General Gavin jumping from the lead aircraft as was his custom. Of these, 2,016 men of 504th Parachute Infantry landed at Grave, including a company of 2/504th dropped deliberately west of the bridge, while 505th Parachute Infantry and 508th Parachute Infantry dropped on to the Groesbeek heights just north and south of the village. The drop included the first ever parachute deployment of artillery into battle by the 544 men of 376th Parachute Artillery Battalion, jumping with their twelve disassembled 75mm howitzers from 48 Dakotas. At about 1330, Browning's I Airborne Corps Headquarters landed near Groesbeek village, without two of its gliders. Finally at 1353, 1st Parachute Brigade jumped west of Arnhem to complete the British landing. By 1408, some 20,000 combat troops, 511 vehicles, 330 artillery pieces and 590 tons of equipment had been safely landed.

As the sky train climbed to 3,000ft (1,000m) for the return journey, Brereton flew back to IX Troop Carrier Command Headquarters at Eastcote (near Moor Park) to oversee the preparations for the second wave next day together with Tedder and Ridgway. Brereton was delighted to have proved that heavy enemy anti-aircraft defences could be overcome to mount a major daylight airborne operation. The whole 'Market' deployment from England was already fixed, and when the second wave flew out next day his role in the battle would effectively be over. There was no one in England to coordinate the land battle with the air plan, and no reserve.

▼ *Men of 1st Airlanding Light Regiment, Royal Artillery, unloading a jeep and trailer from a Horsa glider on Landing Zone 'Z' near Wolfheze, just after touchdown on Sunday 17 September. The tail section of the Horsa was made to detach for ease of unloading. On the left, with red beret, is Lieutenant Colonel W. F. K. 'Sherrif' Thompson, commanding the regiment. Note the signaller in the jeep behind Thompson, already trying to establish a radio net with his 22 radio set, and the wingtip damaged by the glider on landing. (IWM photograph BU1164)*

▶ *Top right: CG-4A Waco gliders of 101st Airborne Division circling and landing north of the Sonsche forest, Sunday 17*

September. This picture gives a good idea of the flatness of the Dutch countryside on either side of the path of XXX Corps' advance. Note that one glider, far right, appears to have ploughed in on landing, breaking its left wingtip and leaving a plume of disturbed earth. (IWM photograph MH2071)

▼ *The C-47 Dakotas of the skytrain turn for home as the last troops of 1st Parachute Brigade land on Drop Zone 'X' near Wolfheze, alongside Horsa gliders that have already been unloaded and abandoned. Note in the background the woods which covered part of the heathland forming 1st British Airborne Division's landing zone. (IWM photograph BU1163)*

THE ALLIED ATTACK, 17 SEPTEMBER

At 1400, with fighter-bombers of RAF 83 Group waiting overhead, Lieutenant General Horrocks' XXX Corps opened its bombardment at Joe's Bridge with eleven field artillery regiments and six medium regiments, a total of 408 guns. After 35 minutes, the Irish Guards Group led off for the Guards Armoured Division along the Club Route up the Eindhoven road, with infantry from 231st Brigade of 50th (Northumbrian) Division keeping pace on either side of the road to widen the bridgehead. Despite Horrocks' fears, the break-through went well, as Kampfgruppe 'Walther' was overwhelmed by the weight of Allied firepower. But Major General Adair, commanding the Guards Armoured, stuck strictly to orders and halted at Valkenswaard at 1930, having lost nine tanks. At the same time, XII Corps under Lieutenant General Ritchie attacked with 15th (Scottish) Division north

from Aart and 53rd (Welsh) Division north from Lommel against Kampfgruppe 'Chill'. Attacking across country without the air support of the Guards, these troops made little progress. Nevertheless, the German defensive crust had been broken, and Field Marshal Montgomery reported to London that XXX Corps would be in Arnhem next day.

North of Eindhoven, 101st Airborne reached most of its objectives by 1600. 501st Parachute Infantry secured the rail and road bridges at Heeswijk and Veghel, and 502nd Parachute Infantry captured the St Oedenrode bridge against light opposition. But at Son, a handful of trainees from the Luftwaffe's Division 'Hermann Goering' blew the bridge over the Wilhelmina Canal as 506th Parachute Infantry arrived, and a weak push by a company of 2/502nd Parachute Infantry towards an alternative bridge south of Best was checked by part of Parachute Battalion 'Jungwirth' (of Kampfgruppe 'Chill'), producing a stalemate. Until bridging equipment from XXX Corps arrived at Son, there was no way forward. Taylor sent foot patrols south towards Eindhoven, but like Adair he made no effort to enter the town.

In response, General Student, watching the landings from his personal headquarters at Vught, redirected 59th Infantry Division from Fifteenth Army, moving eastward by train through Tilburg, to reinforce LXXXVIII Corps at Best. Later that afternoon Student received what he subsequently described as a complete set of plans for 'Market-Garden' from a crashed Allied glider, almost certainly missing from Browning's headquarters. General Hans Reinhard of LXXXVIII Corps ordered Kampfgruppe 'Chill' to hold to the last man, while LXXXVII Corps under General Otto Sponheimer moved 719th Coastal Division eastward to Tournhout in support.

◄ *Soldiers of 231st Infantry Brigade, 50th (Northumbrian) Division, moving up in support of the Guards Armoured Division along the road to Eindhoven from Joe's Bridge on Sunday 17 September. Note the abandoned German 88mm Flak gun by the roadside. Following their retreat, the Germans often lacked the heavy cross-country movers to position these guns properly, and dropped them in exposed positions along the length of the road. This made them easier to overcome, but reinforced the British belief that the Germans had mined the roadside verges, which they had been able to do in only a few places. (IWM photograph B9982)*

Further north still, 82nd Airborne's attempt to capture its bridges also met with mixed fortune. 505th and 508th Parachute Infantry established themselves on either side of Groesbeek village, while 504th Parachute Infantry secured Grave bridge. But two of the three bridges over the Maas-Waal Canal were blown by their German defenders before more troops from 504th and 505th Parachute Infantry arrived on foot. This closed the direct road from Grave to Nijmegen, leaving only the bridge nearest Heumen in American hands. Not until after dark was a single company of 1/508th Parachute Infantry sent into Nijmegen to investigate the road bridge across the River Waal, with the aid of some PAN (Dutch resistance) workers. This was stopped well before the bridge by Kampfgruppe 'Henke', an improvised battalion of soldiers, airmen and railway guards defending Nijmegen.

As the first reports of the landing at Wolfheze came in at 1300, Generalfeldmarschall Model quickly abandoned the Hartenstein Hotel, moving Army Group B Headquarters from Oosterbeek to Terborg, some 50km (30 miles) to the east. At 1330 Obergruppenführer Bittrich at Doetinchem, calling for Brigadeführer Harmel's immediate return from

Market-Garden: Area of Operations, 16-26 Sept 1944

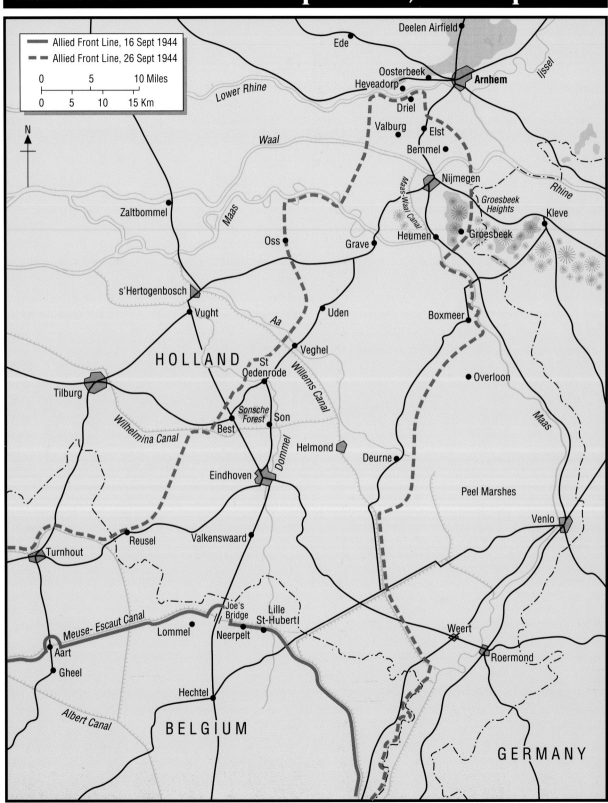

Allied Front Line, 16 Sept 1944
Allied Front Line, 26 Sept 1944

| 0 | 5 | 10 Miles |
| 0 | 5 | 10 | 15 Km |

N

Deelen Airfield
Ede
Oosterbeek
Heveadorp
Arnhem
IJssel
Lower Rhine
Driel
Valburg
Elst
Waal
Bemmel
Rhine
Maas
Nijmegen
Groesbeek
Heights
Kleve
Zaltbommel
Maas-Waal Canal
Oss
Grave
Heumen
Groesbeek
s'Hertogenbosch
Vught
Uden
Boxmeer
Aa
HOLLAND
St
Oedenrode
Veghel
Willems Canal
Overloon
Tilburg
Sonsche
Forest
Son
Best
Maas
Wilhelmina Canal
Helmond
Dommel
Helmond
Deurne
Eindhoven
Peel Marshes
Reusel
Valkenswaard
Venlo
Turnhout
Joe's
Bridge
Lille
St-Hubert
Weert
Meuse- Escaut Canal
Lommel
Neerpelt
Roermond
Aart
Gheel
Hechtel
Albert Canal
BELGIUM
GERMANY

Berlin, ordered his men on to full alert, and SS-Kampfgruppe 'Hohenstauffen' started unloading its remaining vehicles from the trains. At 1500 Model arrived at Doetinchem and assumed direct command of II SS Panzer Corps from Armed Forces Command Netherlands, much to Bittrich's annoyance.

Nevertheless, Model and Bittrich agreed that the key to the battle was not Arnhem, but Nijmegen road bridge. If the Allied drive could be stopped on the Waal, any success farther north became irrelevent. Bittrich wanted to destroy both Arnhem and Nijmegen bridges at once, but Model refused, more aware of Hitler's suspicions and claiming that he needed the bridges for a counter-attack.

At Rastenburg, Hitler was stunned and shaken by the Allied airborne assault. In response to Model's signals he agreed to give the defeat of 'Market-Garden' absolute priority, ranking even above the defence of Germany. Over 300 fighters were promised for next day, virtually the entire Luftwaffe frontline strength in western Europe. Model also obtained the troops in training from Wehrkreiss VI, the military district of Germany immediately east of the Netherlands, together with all those in transit or on leave in the Wesel area, at least 3,000 men formed into improvised march battalions. General Friedrich Christansen in Amsterdam also promised reinforcements from Armed Forces Command Netherlands under his chief training officer, Generalleutnant Hans von Tettau. More importantly, the armour, artillery, ammunition and replacement troops that II SS Panzer Corps badly needed would start to arrive within 48 hours.

The Battle of Arnhem was exactly the kind of military improvisation at which Model excelled, and three hours after the Allied landings his defence plan was ready. General Student was to handle operations near Eindhoven, sending Kampfgruppe 'Chill' against XII Corps and XXX Corps, and 59th Infantry Division together with 107th Panzer Brigade (promised by Generalfeldmarschall Rundstedt at OB West) against 101st Airborne. The forces from Wehrkreiss VI under General Kurt Feldt were to recapture the Groesbeek heights from 82nd Airborne, with II Parachute Corps being rushed from Cologne to assist. SS-Kampfgruppe

'Frundsberg' was to move across Arnhem bridge to Nijmegen that evening and prevent any Allied crossing, while SS-Kampfgruppe 'Hohenstauffen' held the British west of Arnhem. During the battle, Model visited Obersturmbahnführer Harzer's headquarters every day to ensure that reinforcements were getting through.

By 1500, while 1st Airlanding Brigade secured its defensive perimeter around the landing zones west of Arnhem, the British were already in action against 16th SS Panzergrenadier Depot Battalion (440 strong) under Haupsturmführer Sepp Krafft, which had been training on the heath. The SS NCO Training School 'Arnheim' at Wolfheze also formed a scratch force, as did Kampfgruppe 'Weber' of Luftwaffe troops from Deelen. The 3rd Dutch SS Police Battalion was also on its way from the north. The first 47 prisoners the British took came from 27 different parent units.

At about 1540, 1st Parachute Brigade started to move towards Arnhem by three routes, 3rd Battalion of the Parachute Regiment down the main Oosterbeek highway (the 'Lion' route) with the brigade headquarters, led by 28 jeeps of 1st Airborne Reconnaissance Squadron under Major C. F. H. 'Freddie' Gough along the line of the railway, 1st Battalion to the north ('Leopard') and 2nd Battalion to the south ('Tiger'). Most of 1st British Airborne's radios were working, but as expected there were problems in maintaining contact, and divisional headquarters could not reach Gough or Lathbury, who were about to come under heavy fire from Krafft's troops near Oosterbeek. The powerful Luftwaffe transmitter at Deelen, calling for help from all directions, added to the problem.

At about 1600 a false rumour reached Urquhart that most of the gliders carrying Gough's reconnaissance force had failed to arrive. Leaving his headquarters, Urquhart set out to find Gough and check on his division, driving off in his jeep down the 'Lion' route. Reaching part of 2nd Battalion, he failed to find its commander, Lieutenant Colonel John Frost, and swung northwards, meeting Lathbury with 3rd Battalion but away from his own brigade headquarters.

The first part of the paratroops' advance had been almost a triumphal procession beside grateful Dutch civilians. Now, among the trees and buildings on the outskirts of Oosterbeek, they encountered increasing numbers of German snipers and mortar teams, and Urquhart's own jeep was hit. 1st Battalion to the north was having equal trouble as Obersturmbahnführer Harzer assembled his blocking force, SS-Kampfgruppe 'Spindler' (barely two battalions) which gradually absorbed Krafft's troops into a solid line by midnight, cutting off 1st Parachute Brigade from Arnhem bridge and the high ground. As darkness fell, Urquhart radioed to his headquarters that he and Lathbury were spending the night with 3rd Battalion.

Meanwhile, Major Gough had heard that he was wanted and, returning to divisional headquarters, found that Urquhart had gone. He set out once more towards Arnhem. At about 1900 one of

▼ *The body of General-major Kussin in his bullet-ridden staff car, caught in a hail of fire by men of 3rd Battalion of the Parachute Regiment at Wolfheze crossroads, taken by a member of the* *Army Film and Photographic Unit on the evening of Sunday 17 September. Two of Kussin's aides who were with him in the car also died. (IWM photograph BU1155)*

Gough's patrols notified 1st British Airborne Headquarters of the existence of a ferry at Heveadorp, but with Urquhart elsewhere no action was taken to secure the ferry.

On the German side, at about 1800 Generalmajor Kussin, the Arnhem Town Commandant who was responsible for the defence of its bridges, was killed by paratroops of 3rd Battalion at Wolfheze crossroads after driving to confer with Krafft. As Frost's 2nd Battalion approached the railway bridge at about 1830 it was blown in their faces, and the pontoon bridge was found to be dismantled as expected. But at Arnhem road bridge itself the small guard of German pioneer troops had abandoned their posts, and the bridge was undefended. Approaching at dusk, the paratroops watched 30 vehicles of 9th SS Reconnaissance Battalion drive on to the bridge from the north, and keep going: the battalion was on loan to SS-Kampfgruppe 'Frundsberg', and its orders were to drive to Nijmegen. At 1930 the first of Frost's men moved completely unopposed into position among the buildings at the northern end of the bridge. Within half an hour the first troops of the 'Frundsberg' heading for Nijmegen tried to cross the bridge from the north and found their way blocked.

Bittrich at once secured the southern end of the bridge with armoured cars of 10th SS Reconnaissance Battalion. Frost did not have enough troops to hold the entire bridge, and a speculative night attack with flamethrowers on a German pillbox at the northern end did little but set most of the structure alight. But before night fell, Frost notified divisional headquarters and Urquhart that his end of the bridge was secure.

During the night Major Gough reached the bridge with two of his jeeps, and other troops of 1st Parachute Brigade managed to get through to Frost before dawn. By morning his force was about 600 men, mostly from his own 2nd Battalion, including four 6pdr anti-tank guns plus mortars and anti-tank mines. More importantly, at 0800 the headquarters of 1st Parachute Brigade arrived (without Lathbury), giving Frost radio contact with 1st British Airborne Headquarters and artillery support from one of the three troops (four guns each) of the division's 75mm howitzers.

THE ALLIED FAILURE, 18 SEPTEMBER

The Allied meteorologists were one day out in their predictions, and on Monday (D plus 1) the autumn weather closed down. Heavy fog in the morning was followed by heavy rain in the afternoon and evening. In England, the take-off of the second airborne wave, due for dawn at 0600, was delayed. The fog also grounded the Allied aircraft in Belgium and northern France for the morning. Lieutenant General Ridgway flew out to Brussels in an effort to join his troops but was unable to land because of the weather. Farther north in Holland and western Germany the airfields cleared just as the Luftwaffe started its maximum effort. Together with Browning's failure to arrange RAF and USAAF liaison officers with his troops, and Brereton's stipulation that the aircraft in Belgium remain grounded while his own were flying, this meant that 82nd Airborne received only 97 close-support sorties from RAF 83 Group, and 1st British Airborne received none, compared with 190 Luftwaffe fighters committed to the area. German air attacks took place as far south as Joe's Bridge, which was narrowly missed by a fighter-bomber raid. 'Market-Garden', a plan based on air power, was the only battle of the entire campaign in North-West Europe fought with Allied air inferiority, a large part of it self-inflicted.

At 0600, with the armoured cars of the 2nd Household Cavalry Regiment reconnoitring ahead, the Guards Armoured advance resumed, leaving 231st Brigade to hold Valkenswaard. Halfway to Eindhoven the Grenadier Guards Group took over

▶ *Humber armoured cars of 2nd Household Cavalry Regiment driving through the streets of Eindhoven, Monday 18 September. A composite unit made up from the Life Guards and the Royal Horse Guards, the Household were known in radio communication by their collective regimental nickname of the 'Stable Boys', and acted as the reconnaissance battalion for XXX Corps during the battle. (IWM photograph B10127A)*

the lead, with the Welsh Guards Group opening up the second Heart Route axis towards Helmond. During the morning, 506th Parachute Infantry cleared Eindhoven of a single German company and secured the bridges over the River Dommel east of the town. By the evening, the Guards Armoured had passed around east of Eindhoven and reached the destroyed bridge at Son, where work on a Bailey bridge began. The Welsh Guards' attempt to strike out across country had bogged down against Kampfgruppe 'Walther' in the flat terrain, and Major General Adair ordered it to rejoin the main axis at Son.

During the day, German LXXXVI Corps arrived from the east under General Hans von Obstfelder with 176th Infantry Division (7,000 trainees and semi-invalids) and Division 'Erdmann' (3,000 recruits for the planned 7th Parachute Division), strengthening the German position between Weert and Helmond. Meanwhile, after a strong attempt by 2/502nd and 3/502nd Parachute Infantry to capture Best bridge, it was finally blown at 1100 by 59th Infantry Division. The British advance now depended entirely on the speed at which the Bailey bridge at Son was completed.

With dawn at Nijmegen, Gavin ordered 1/508th and 3/508th Parachute Infantry to try again for the road bridge. Three times during the day the paratroops reported that the bridge was theirs, but each time the German defence held. Blocked at Arnhem bridge, SS-Kampfgruppe 'Frundsberg' began the slow process of ferrying troops and vehicles across the Pannerdern Canal, the canalized stretch of the Lower Rhine east of Arnhem. The first troops reached Nijmegen on bicycles, followed by four PzKpfw IV tanks, the vanguard of SS-Kampfgruppe 'Reinhold'. Brigade-führer Harmel, who had driven flat-out from Berlin, set up headquarters next day at Doornesberg 9km (six miles) north of Nijmegen to coordinate the defence.

Also at dawn, the first troops of Corps 'Feldt' from Wehrkreis VI, about 3,400 barely trained men in four groups under 406th Landesschütz Division, started to attack on the Groesbeek heights, finding gaps in the thin American line. During the day, the PAN warned Gavin of more Germans massing in the Reichswald. Taking this to heart,

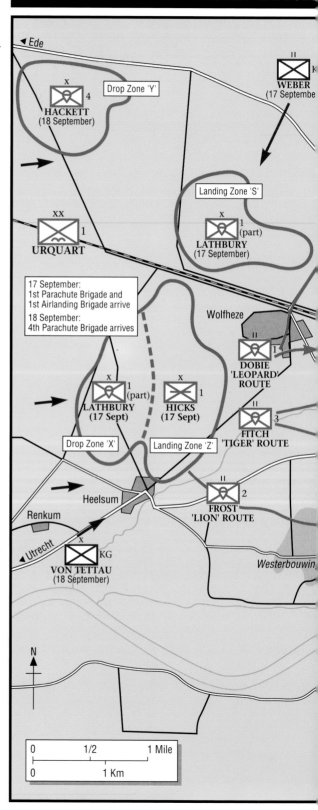

Arnhem: Britis

Airborne Division Operations, 17-21 September 1944

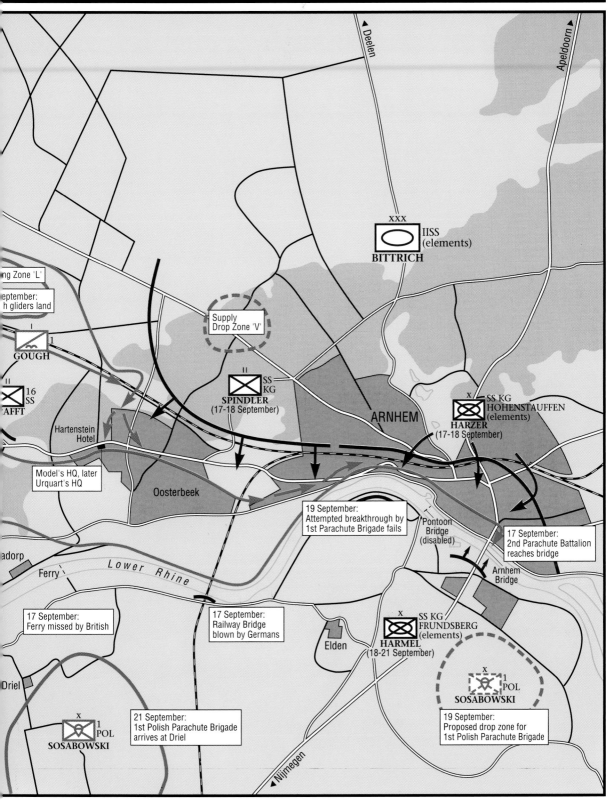

Deelen

Apeldoorn

XXX IISS (elements)
BITTRICH

ng Zone 'L'

eptember:
h gliders land

I 1
GOUGH

Supply Drop Zone 'V'

II
16 SS
AFFT

II SS KG
SPINDLER
(17-18 September)

ARNHEM

X SS KG HOHENSTAUFFEN (elements)
HARZER
(17-18 September)

Hartenstein Hotel

Model's HQ, later Urquart's HQ

Oosterbeek

19 September:
Attempted breakthrough by
1st Parachute Brigade fails

Pontoon Bridge (disabled)

17 September:
2nd Parachute Battalion reaches bridge

adorp

Ferry

Lower Rhine

Arnhem Bridge

17 September:
Ferry missed by British

17 September:
Railway Bridge
blown by Germans

Elden

X SS KG FRUNDSBERG (elements)
HARMEL
(18-21 September)

Drirl

X 1 POL
SOSABOWSKI

19 September:
Proposed drop zone for
1st Polish Parachute Brigade

X 1 POL
SOSABOWSKI

21 September:
1st Polish Parachute Brigade
arrives at Driel

Nijmegen

◀ *Men of 'C' Troop of Major Gough's 1st Airborne Reconnaissance Squadron near Wolfheze station on Monday 18 September, with their jeeps just visible beyond the railway line. The soldier in the foreground is armed with a PIAT. This picture gives a good idea of the woodland between the British landing zones and Oosterbeek. (IWM photograph BU1144)*

▼ *The result of the attack by 9th SS Reconnaissance Battalion of the 'Hohenstauffen' across Arnhem bridge into*

Frost's position, taken by an RAF reconnaissance aircraft on Monday 18 September, looking east. The picture shows the raised section of the main road leading on to the bridge itself (to the right of the picture). Over twenty destroyed German half-tracks and reconnaissance vehicles can be seen. Haupsturmführer Viktor Grabner, commanding the battalion, who had received the Knight's Cross from Obersturmbahnführer Harzer at noon on the previous day, was killed in the attack. (IWM photograph MH2062)

▼ *Lieutenant Colonel John Frost was the most experienced battalion commander in 1st British Airborne Division, having commanded 2nd Battalion of the Parachute Regiment since October 1942 and led it through battles in North Africa and Sicily. Like all British paratroops, he was a volunteer. He is shown here as a major in the uniform of his parent regiment, the Cameronians (Scottish Rifles), after receiving the Military Cross for leading the Bruneval Raid of 27 February 1942, the Parachute Regiment's first Battle Honour.*

82nd Airborne and Browning with them fought the rest of the battle for Nijmegen bridge looking over one shoulder, preparing to defend against an expected armoured drive by II SS Panzer Corps across the Groesbeek heights which never came.

At Arnhem, both sides attacked before dawn. Kampfgruppe 'von Tettau' (including 224th Panzer Company with French Renault tanks) moved against 1st Airlanding Brigade from Renkum to the west, gradually aborbing all other German forces west of Oosterbeek in a firefight that lasted most of the day. Meanwhile, 3rd Battalion of the Parachute Regiment resumed its advance towards Arnhem bridge against SS-Kampfgruppe 'Spindler', with Lathbury and Urquhart in attendance.

As 3rd Battalion's advance pushed to within 2,000m of the bridge, the British and Germans became intermingled in confused street fighting. Urquhart's party was cut off, and shortly before noon Lathbury was wounded and had to be left in a nearby house. As the Germans closed in, Urquhart accompanied by two captains was forced to take refuge in a sympathetic householder's attic while enemy troops patrolled the streets below. With Urquhart and Lathbury both missing, Brigadier Hicks officially took over the division at 0915, sending 2nd Battalion of the South Staffordshire Regiment (two companies strong) to reinforce 1st Parachute Brigade's increasingly fragmented drive.

At Arnhem bridge itself, Frost was still in a strong position, with at least as many troops as SS-Kampfgruppe 'Knaust' of the 'Hohenstauffen', which attacked from the north. The Germans soon discovered that the airborne troops were a formidable enemy, and that infantry assaults achieved little against them. Artillery and armour were needed to blast Frost's men out of their houses, and two 100mm guns began the process just after dawn. At 0930 about 22 vehicles of 9th SS Reconnaissance Battalion returned from Nijmegen and tried to charge across the bridge and into Frost's position, only to be destroyed by British mines, anti-tank guns and grenades. But Frost had rations only for 48 hours, and was forced to restrict ammunition during the day. Meanwhile, 1st Parachute Brigade was checked by SS-Kampfgruppe 'Spindler' still short of the bridge. Over the next two days the replacement tanks and guns demanded by Model

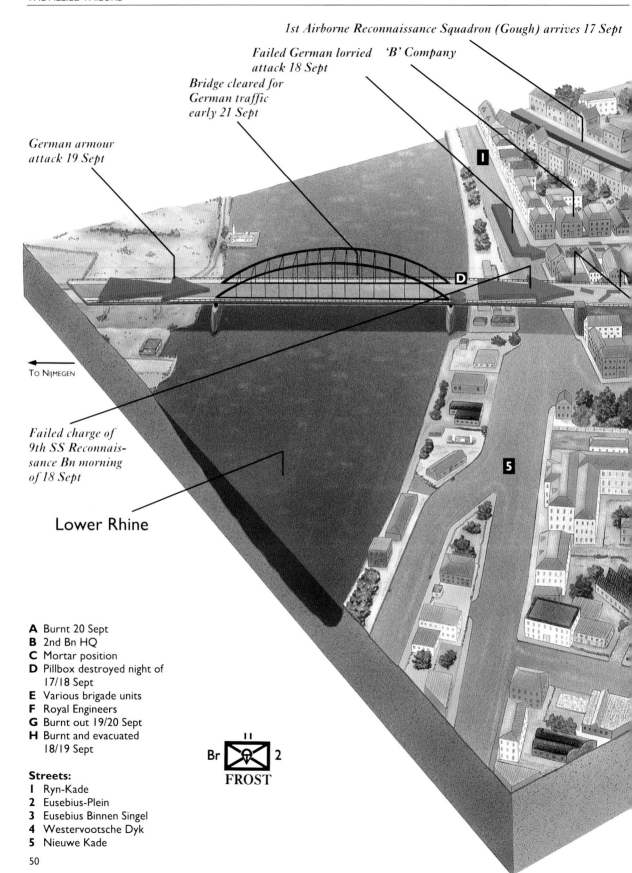

1st Airborne Reconnaissance Squadron (Gough) arrives 17 Sept

Failed German lorried attack 18 Sept

'B' Company

Bridge cleared for German traffic early 21 Sept

German armour attack 19 Sept

I

D

To Nijmegen

Failed charge of 9th SS Reconnaissance Bn morning of 18 Sept

Lower Rhine

5

A Burnt 20 Sept
B 2nd Bn HQ
C Mortar position
D Pillbox destroyed night of 17/18 Sept
E Various brigade units
F Royal Engineers
G Burnt out 19/20 Sept
H Burnt and evacuated 18/19 Sept

Streets:
1 Ryn-Kade
2 Eusebius-Plein
3 Eusebius Binnen Singel
4 Westervootsche Dyk
5 Nieuwe Kade

Br 2
FROST

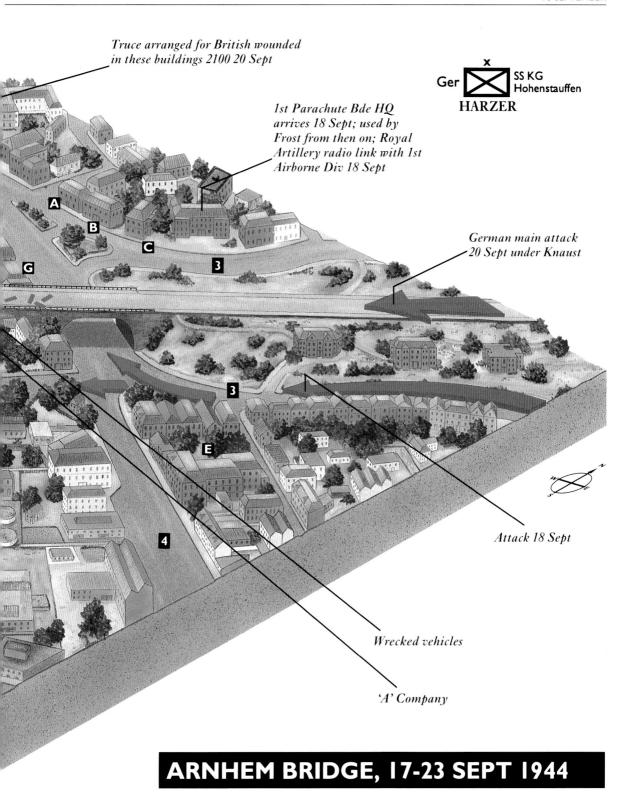

Truce arranged for British wounded
in these buildings 2100 20 Sept

1st Parachute Bde HQ
arrives 18 Sept; used by
Frost from then on; Royal
Artillery radio link with 1st
Airborne Div 18 Sept

Ger **SS KG**
Hohenstauffen
HARZER

A

B

C

G

3

German main attack
20 Sept under Knaust

3

E

4

Attack 18 Sept

Wrecked vehicles

'A' Company

ARNHEM BRIDGE, 17-23 SEPT 1944

**Frost's men held the northern part of the bridge, denying the
Germans a crossing place, until the night of 20/21 Sept. The
last British resistance near the bridge ceased 23 Sept**

started to arrive at Arnhem from all over Germany, including Flak Brigade 'Von Swoboda' from Luftwaffe West equipped with 70 anti-aircraft guns (33 x 88mm, 29 x 20mm and 8 x 37mm) in five battalions.

All this was unknown to Browning and his staff, who were rapidly discovering the difference between an administrative headquarters and an Army Corps command. There was endless trouble with radio communications, for which Browning later blamed his signals section. In fact the GHQ Liaison Regiment ('Phantom') unit with 1st British Airborne was in touch with London through its specialist radio equipment, as was a BBC reporting team with a VHS set (later in the battle, newspapers carrying their first reports were dropped to the troops at Arnhem), and the division had direct contact with Frost on Arnhem bridge. 1st British Airborne was also speaking to I Airborne Corps Rear Headquarters at Moor Park, which was in intermittent contact with Browning. The PAN, using a private telephone system belonging to the regional electricity company, also sent coded messages between Arnhem and Nijmegen warning 82nd Airborne that 1st British Airborne was in

trouble, and the same telephone system reached south to 101st Airborne at Son. The failure was not principally one of communications, but of staffwork and experience at Browning's headquarters. Next morning I Airborne Corps asked Moor Park for copies of 1st British Airborne's signals, and that afternoon firm radio contact was established. But for the vital first two days of the battle, Browning was never in proper command.

At 1000 in England, the glider/tug combinations of the delayed second airlift took off, followed by the paratroop carriers at 1200, all in one stream on the northern route escorted by 867 fighters of 8th Air Force and Fighter Command. In the bad weather, 91 out of 904 gliders taking off failed to arrive or were lost over Holland. At 1300 two battalions of 327th Glider Infantry Regiment and some divisional troops, a total of 2,656 men, 146 jeeps, 109 trailers and two bulldozers, reached 101st Airborne safely in 428 gliders, and Major General Taylor ordered his deputy, Brigadier General Gerald Higgins (at 34, the youngest general in the US Army) to take over the western flank of his defences. Within the hour, 502nd Parachute Infantry reinforced by British tanks from 8th

◀ *The British Army's backpacked 68P radio set (shown here being worn by a Polish paratrooper) was used for speech over a range of about 5km (three miles). The two jeep-mounted sets, the 22 set and the 19HP set, had ranges of 8km (five miles) and 40km (25 miles) respectively. Beyond this, the 76 Morse key set with a range of 500km (300 miles) was used. Throughout the war, radio communications were intermittent in all battles, and likely to fail altogether at night.*

▲ *Receiving neither jump pay nor flight pay, American glider troops were sensitive to their undeserved image as inferior to the paratroopers with whom they shared equal dangers. Here troops of* *327th Gilder Infantry Regiment, 101st Airborne Division, attempt to clear the bodies and wreckage from a CG-4A Waco glider after a particularly heavy landing near Son on Monday 18 September.*

Armoured Brigade attacked 59th Infantry Division's positions at Best and took more than 1,400 prisoners; the village itself remained in German hands. Farther north, a probe by 59th Infantry Division towards Veghel was beaten off by the Americans.

On Groesbeek heights the morning attack by Corps 'Feldt' had overrun part of 82nd Airborne's landing zones, which were cleared in a rifle charge by 505th Parachute Infantry just as 385 gliders landed with 1,782 men and the remainder of the division's artillery (twelve 75mm guns, twelve 105mm guns and eight 57mm anti-tank guns) at

1300, almost capturing General Feldt himself. As the tug aircraft departed, 135 B-25 Liberators of 8th Air Force dropped resupply to 82nd Airborne (80 per cent of which was recovered) and a further 117 Liberators dropped resupply to 101st Airborne (50 per cent recovered), losing eleven aircraft. At 1700 Browning ordered Gavin to plan for a night attack on Nijmegen bridge, then changed his mind and cancelled the attack.

West of Arnhem the British second wave arrived at 1500 to heavy German anti-aircraft fire which set fire to the heath below them. Hackett's 4th Parachute Brigade, in 124 Dakotas, dropped from 800ft (250m) right on top of 3rd Dutch SS Police Battalion, which was skirmishing with 1st Airlanding Brigade, causing the Dutch SS to rout. The remainder of the South Staffordshire Regiment and the rest of the divisional troops also landed in 296 gliders, a total of 2,119 men. Only one Dakota was lost, but 20 escorting fighters were shot down holding off 90 Luftwaffe aircraft.

This landing was followed by 145 Stirlings and

Dakotas of RAF 38 and 46 Group on resupply. But the intended supply drop zone was still in German hands, and the Germans copied the British recognition signals. Most of the aircraft were hit by anti-aircraft fire, and of 87 tons dropped only twelve tons reached 1st British Airborne, for the loss of thirteen aircraft.

On landing, Hackett was surprised to be told by Mackenzie that Hicks was commanding the division, and was taking away 11th Battalion of the Parachute Regiment and the South Staffordshires to reinforce 1st Parachute Brigade's attack. Hackett arrived at the Hartenstein Hotel, now established as 1st British Airborne's headquarters, shortly before midnight, where Hicks ordered him to send his remaining two battalions at once up alongside 1st Parachute Brigade towards Arnhem. Hackett protested that he needed a plan, and that his brigade should attack towards its original objective of the high ground. A heated exchange followed in which Hicks accused Hackett of trying to take the division from him, but finally agreed to a delay.

The absence of the commander of 1st British Airborne at this point was critical. What mattered was a bridgehead over the Lower Rhine. If Hicks had given up the original objective of Arnhem

bridge he could have secured the Heveadorp ferry and the ground on either side, dug in and waited for XXX Corps. But this would have meant disobeying Browning's orders, and abandoning Frost.

With the junction between XXX Corps and 101st Airborne complete, Major General Taylor came under Horrocks' command. In turn, 50th (Northumbrian) Division was passed to VIII Corps under Lieutenant General O'Connor and began to move up towards Eindhoven. Just on midnight, VIII Corps began its delayed supporting attack with an assault crossing of the Meuse-Escaut Canal at Lille St Hubert by 3rd Division, part of which was still on the road from Brussels.

After two days, the battle was starting to swing against Montgomery. Despite breaking through the German defences, XXX Corps was checked at Son while the two flanking Army Corps had yet to make an impact. I Airborne Corps had lost any advantage of surprise from its airborne assault and had fallen into disarray. There was little information available to 21st Army Group on which to base an assessment, and no British reserve with which to influence the battle.

On the other side, Model's counter-attack was now ready.

◀ *Brigadier 'Pip' Hicks, taken at his headquarters at the Hartenstein Hotel on Monday 18 September. Hicks, who celebrated his 49th birthday during the battle (the same age as Lieutenant General Horrocks), was probably the oldest brigade commander in the British Army. He had led 1st Airlanding Brigade since April 1943, including its first major battle in the liberation of Sicily. (IWM photograph BU1152)*

THE GERMAN COUNTER-ATTACK, 19 SEPTEMBER

On Tuesday (D plus 2) the weather continued with fog in the morning and rain all day. The third wave of flights from England, due to take off at 1000, was fogbound until 1300 when the last battalion of 327th Glider Infantry took off with 101st Airborne's artillery in 385 gliders, of which 189 were lost or turned back. The 428 gliders carrying 82nd Airborne's reinforcement, chiefly two battalions of 325th Glider Infantry, remained grounded all day. The 114 Dakotas of 1st Polish Parachute Brigade were also grounded, but the brigade's small component of 35 gliders took off alone.

News of these changes was not passed by First Allied Airborne Army to 2nd Tactical Air Force in Belgium, which continued to fly support according to the original timetable. As a result, the airborne troops in Holland received no close air support, compared to 125 Luftwaffe fighter sorties. During the day, 43 Allied aircraft and 73 gliders were lost. Considering his job complete, Lieutenant General Brereton flew to Brussels with Ridgway and drove on to Eindhoven, wearing his dress uniform complete with medals, to watch the victory.

At 0330 in the dark and fog at Arnhem, 1st Parachute Brigade started its attack eastward along the line of the Lower Rhine, while 4th Parachute Brigade (10th and 156th Battalions of the Parachute Regiment) moved north-east across the railway line towards the high ground. 1st Parachute Brigade made about 400m towards the bridge before the fog lifted shortly after dawn, when it found itself caught in a German crossfire on the river road, between 20mm multi-barrelled anti-aircraft guns firing from the southern bank and SS-Kampfgruppe 'Spindler' from the embankment to the north. By 1000 the British attack had collapsed and been routed. At the

▶ *Paratroops of 1st Polish Parachute Brigade waiting beside their grounded C-47 Dakota at an airfield in eastern England, probably Tuesday 19 September. In Browning's plan, all German anti-aircraft defences to the south of Arnhem bridge would have been overcome by this date, making it safe to land paratroops. Major General Sosabowski made little effort to hide his lack of enthusiasm for this plan, or his belief that his troops were being misused by Browning.*

◀ *Men of the 2nd Battalion of the South Staffordshires moving down the main road from their landing zone through Oosterbeek to Arnhem on the morning of Tuesday 19 September, together with a 6pdr anti-tank gun towed by a jeep. Like all British airlanding troops, the South Staffordshires were a line battalion that had received special training in gliders. Note the woodland on either side of the road, which both sides found perfect for ambushes. (IWM photograph BU1091)*

end of the day, 1st Battalion of the Parachute Regiment numbered 40 unwounded men, while 3rd Battalion escaped with 116 men.

The attack through the town by 11th Battalion of the Parachute Regiment and 2nd Battalion of the South Staffordshires also met little success, reducing them to about 150 and 200 men respectively in the day's fighting. But by 0715 they had driven SS-Kampfgruppe 'Spindler' back far enough to free Major General Urquhart from his attic. Urquhart reached the Hartenstein minutes later by jeep, and began to reorganize what remained of his division. Hackett's attack north-east was reinforced by 7th Battalion of the King's Own Scottish Borderers from 1st Airlanding Brigade, leaving only 1st Battalion of the Border Regiment in reserve. Warnings were broadcast to 1st Polish Parachute Brigade not to land on its planned zones, which were under German control. Urquhart also ordered Colonel Hilary Barlow, deputy commander of 1st Airlanding Brigade, to take command of the street battle in Arnhem. Barlow set off towards the fighting and was never seen again, alive or dead. Years later, his battered cigarette case was found less than 1,000m from Arnhem bridge.

At Son, the Bailey bridge was complete, and the Guards Armoured resumed their advance at dawn. By 0820 the Household Cavalry reached Grave bridge, where Browning and Gavin were waiting for Horrocks, with the Grenadiers arriving two hours later. The journey of 85km (53 miles) from Joe's Bridge to Nijmegen had taken the Guards Armoured 42 hours and 130 casualties.

The arrival of XXX Corps put 82nd Airborne under Horrocks, who was increasingly unwell, and left Browning commanding only 1st British Airborne, with which he was barely in contact. The two Army Corps commanders, with Gavin and Adair, set up a joint HQ near Heumen and pro-ceeded to command by a form of mutual agreement.

With 325th Glider Infantry delayed, Gavin had organized 450 of his glider pilots into an improvised battalion and was grateful for support from 8th Armoured Brigade and the Guards Armoured. An attack by 2/505th Parachute Infantry with the Grenadiers at Nijemegen began that afternoon but again failed to reach the bridge. Gavin proposed an assault crossing of the Waal to take the bridge from both ends, and Horrocks ordered XXX Corps' assault boats forward from Hechtel, through the

▶ *A 75mm pack howitzer of 1st Airlanding Light Artillery Regiment in action at Oosterbeek, Tuesday 19 September. Of American manufacture, the howitzer had an effective range of approximately 9,500m and a weight of 500kg (1,200lb). The radio communications and fire support of these guns were vital to Frost's defence of Arnhem bridge. (IWM photograph BU1094)*

rest of the traffic strung out on the highway.

East of Son, 107th Panzer Brigade (a battalion of PzKpfw V Panther tanks and a regiment of panzergrenadiers) arrived for Student's planned pincer attack with 59th Infantry Division from Best. This was pre-empted early in the afternoon by a renewed attack by 101st Airborne and 8th Armoured Brigade which routed 59th Infantry Division north of Best, securing 1,400 prisoners. 107th Panzer Brigade attacked by itself later in the afternoon from the east across the difficult country and almost overran 101st Airborne's headquarters at Son before Taylor could improvise a successful defence. While this was happening, 196 gliders landed with half Taylor's expected artillery and 1,341 out of 2,310 troops, followed by 60 Dakotas which delivered only 40 out of 256 tons of stores on target.

At Arnhem, by mid-afternoon the fighting had been continuous for 48 hours, and 1st British Airborne's attack was being ground down by lack of supplies, high casualties and sheer exhaustion. More German armour and artillery were arriving all the time, including 208th Assault Brigade (Sturm-geschütz IIIs) from Denmark and the first guns of

Flak Brigade 'Von Swoboda'. Neither General-leutnant von Tettau to the west nor Ober-sturmbahnführer Harzer to the east had a clear picture of the battle, or could coordinate their own forces, but 4th Parachute Brigade found its drive north-east firmly blocked.

Under fire from SS-Kampfgruppe 'Krafft' and threatened from the west, Hackett began to pull his brigade back south of the railway line at 1600. Just at this moment the Polish gliders arrived without an escort and landed between the British and German forces on their planned landing zone, having failed to receive Urquhart's warning. Only two Polish anti-tank guns and a handful of men survived to join the British. By the end of the day, Hackett's three battalions each numbered about 250 men. Resupply aircraft of RAF 38 and 46 Group following the Poles, 63 Dakotas and 100 Stirlings, dropped only 31 out of 390 tons correctly to 1st British Airborne, losing thirteen aircraft.

On Arnhem bridge, the day began with a German air raid, followed by shells and mortars from SS-Kampfgruppe 'Knaust' to the north and SS-Kampfgruppe 'Brinkmann' to the east. Frost now had only 250 unwounded men in ten of the eighteen houses he had first occupied. Protecting the wounded and prisoners was becoming a critical problem, as were food, water and ammunition. The battle for Arnhem bridge had become a waking nightmare in which the troops lost track of time. The Germans continued to blast the British out of their positions, but every time they attacked they were driven back, and the bridge remained closed. A summons to Frost to surrender was contempt-uously rejected.

On the left flank of XXX Corps' drive towards Arnhem, 53rd Division of XII Corps had exhausted itself reaching the Turnhout-Eindhoven road. 7th

Armoured Division took over the Aart bridgehead, and 15th Division sidestepped eastward to pass through 53rd Division next day. On the right flank, 3rd Division of VIII Corps had almost reached Weert, and 11th Armoured Division had passed through towards Helmond, reaching just south-east of Eindhoven. The pressure on 101st Airborne led Dempsey to reinforce Taylor with a further armoured battalion from VIII Corps' 4th Armoured Brigade.

As dusk fell, the Luftwaffe bombed Eindhoven with 120 Ju 87s and Ju 88s (its only long-range bombing raid of autumn 1944 in Western Europe), causing at least 1,000 civilian casualties. Brereton and Ridgway, who had just arrived in the town by jeep, were caught up in the bombing and separated. Next morning Ridgway pressed on northwards to meet Taylor and Gavin at their respective headquarters. Brereton went separately to see Taylor at Son before turning back, and flew next day to SHAEF Headquarters to attend a planning conference, making no further effort to influence the battle.

▼ *A PzKpfw V Ausf. G Panther, probably of 9th SS Panzer Regiment, 9th SS Panzer Division 'Hohenstauffen', during the retreat through France to Arnhem. The tank is heavily camou-flaged against Allied air attack, with a lot of external stowage, and two of the crew are performing aircraft sentry duty. A quick camouflage scheme of brown and green patches has been painted over the factory yellow, and no markings are visible except for the prominent (and puzz-ling) '6' on the turret.*

THE STALEMATE, 20 SEPTEMBER

The fog and rain continued into Wednesday (D plus 3), grounding the Poles and 325th Glider Infantry in England once again. Only resupply drops were possible, and 82nd Airborne received 80 per cent of its supplies. By dawn Urquhart had pulled 4th Parachute Brigade back and assembled his division into a thumb-shaped pocket at Oosterbeek with its base on the Lower Rhine. Using the Phantom radio equipment, Urquhart agreed with I Airborne Corps that the Poles should now land at Driel, opposite the Heveadorp ferry, to establish a bridgehead. Urquhart got through on the BBC radio to change 1st British Airborne's supply drop zones, but dropping canisters into the woods and streets of Oosterbeek against the intense German anti-aircraft fire was haphazard, and only thirteen per cent of its intended supplies reached 1st British Airborne.

Uncoordinated German attacks continued all the way around the British perimeter at Oosterbeek, with the forces intermingled in the woods and houses. An attack shortly after dawn by Kampfgruppe 'von Tettau' and SS-Kampfgruppe 'Krafft' against the perimeter was heavily repulsed. With neither side strong enough to make a decisive attack the fighting began to slow down, largely from exhaustion, into an affair of snipers and mortars. In at least one house the British and Germans held different floors and passed rations to each other, while 1st British Airborne found time during the battle to produce a one-sheet newspaper.

But this slowing of the pace did nothing to diminish the casualties. By the end of the day no Parachute Regiment battalion numbered more than 100 men, and only 1st Battalion of the Border Regiment was still intact. Within the perimeter both movement and care of the wounded became impossible, with the Main Dressing Stations coming under fire. By agreement the British pulled back slightly at mid-day to give the Germans possession of these buildings, allowing them to tend the

▶ *Soldiers of 101st Airborne take cover as a convoy of XXX Corps trucks comes under German fire on 'Hell's Highway' north of Eindhoven, Wednesday 20 September. The American defence was handicapped by all their movement being cross-country, as the road was reserved for the British. Although they were mostly unsuccessful, the delays imposed by these German attacks on XXX Corps' movement up the road helped decide the battle. (IWM photograph BU1062)*

wounded properly. This was one of several incidents of cooperation between enemies in a very hard-fought battle. Model further ordered that all civilians in Arnhem and Oosterbeek, which were now in a battle zone, were to be evacuated, which took four days to complete. The 'Orange Battalion' of the PAN with 1st British Airborne, some of whom fought at Arnhem bridge, quietly disbanded next day.

North of Eindhoven, on what 101st Airborne had started to call 'Hell's Highway', the German attacks began again at dawn. 107th Panzer Brigade advanced once more from the east against Son but was beaten back by 101st Airborne with British armoured support. Taylor then switched to a limited offensive, and 1/501st Parachute Infantry at Heeswijk took 418 German prisoners.

While 101st Airborne and 8th Armoured Brigade fought, XXX Corps continued up the road as best it could, including the delayed assault boats and 43rd (Wessex) Division moving from Hechtel. The first troops of the division's 130th Brigade reached Grave at noon, but on the congested road the full division took even longer than the Guards Armoured to reach Nijmegen.

At I Airborne Corps Headquarters the delays on Hell's Highway together with the news from Arnhem caused Gavin to snap at Horrocks' slowness, while the normally icy Browning threw an ink bottle at a picture of a German general on the wall. Help was offered by 52nd (Lowland) Division, which volunteered to fly into an airstrip near Nijmegen next day. Browning, still expecting the Poles and 325th Glider Infantry, turned the offer down.

Because of 82nd Airborne's weakness and the expected major attack at Groesbeek, the Guards Armoured was broken up to provide support. While the Grenadiers and Irish Guards prepared for the assault crossing, the Welsh Guards covered Grave bridge, and the Coldstream supported the Groesbeek position. Meanwhile the Household Cavalry patrolled west as far as the main supply depot for First Parachute Army at Oss, where the pragmatic storekeepers issued supplies to both sides (German rations from Oss reached as far south as British 3rd Division at Weert during the battle).

That morning, the Irish Guards and 504th Parachute Infantry started to clear the suburbs of Nijmegen for the river crossing, while the Grenadiers and 505th Parachute Infantry moved towards the bridge. The assault crossing began at 1440, just after the arrival of the boats, with an attack by Typhoons of RAF 83 Group, followed by a ten-minute artillery and smoke bombardment from 100 guns of XXX Corps and the tanks of the Irish Guards. At 1500 two companies of 3/504th Parachute Infantry crossed the Waal west of the bridges in 19ft assault boats under heavy German artillery fire. Half the boats reached the far shore, and six successive journeys brought the rest of 3/504th Parachute Infantry and 1/504th Parachute Infantry across. Once ashore, 3/504th Parachute Infantry attacked eastwards, clearing first the railway bridge

▶ *Cromwell tanks of the Guards Armoured Division, heavily festooned with external baggage, driving up 'Hell's Highway' just south of Nijmegen, Wednesday 20 September. The windmills in the area were used to pump water along the nearby drainage ditches. Throughout the battle, the last vehicles of a division moving up the road to Arnhem were at least 24 hours behind its leading troops. (IWM photograph B10131)*

then the road bridge at the cost of 107 casualties. Some 417 German bodies were later recovered from the railway bridge area alone. At the same time, 505th Parachute Infantry and the Grenadiers attacked through the town towards the road bridge, the first Grenadier tanks crossing at 1910. In defiance of Model's orders, Brigadeführer Harmel ordered the bridge blown as the Grenadiers crossed, but the charges failed to go off. Later that night Model, not realizing he was too late, author-ized Bittrich to blow Nijmegen bridge if necessary.

On Groesbeek heights, Corps 'Feldt' resumed its attack at dawn with 406th Landesschützen Division to the north and the newly arrived II Parachute Corps to the south. Serving under General Feldt, this consisted of the Training Battalions of 3rd and 5th Parachute Divisions, both of which had been destroyed in Normandy. By mid-morning 82nd Airborne had identified this attack as coming from both full strength parachute divisions and alerted Gavin, who returned to his command post from Nijmegen. At first II Parachute Corps' drive met considerable success, and by evening it had almost reached the bridge at Heumen, threatening to cut the road behind 82nd Airborne. But counter-attacks by 508th Parachute Infantry, supported by the Coldstream, gradually restored the position.

At Arnhem bridge, Frost had water for only one more day, and Urquhart advised I Airborne Corps

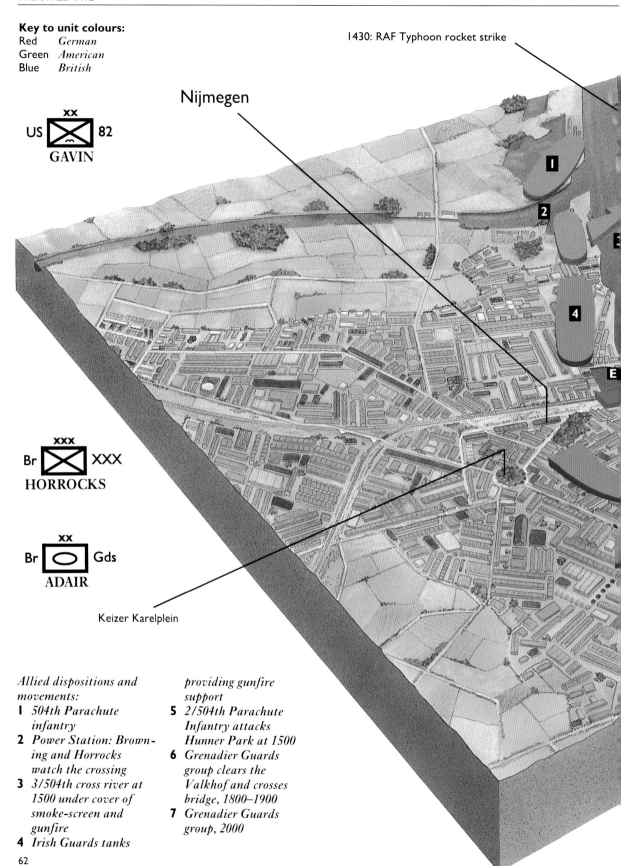

Key to unit colours:
Red *German*
Green *American*
Blue *British*

1430: RAF Typhoon rocket strike

US ⊠ 82
GAVIN

Nijmegen

Br ⊠ XXX
HORROCKS

Br ◯ Gds
ADAIR

Keizer Karelplein

Allied dispositions and movements:
1 *504th Parachute infantry*
2 *Power Station: Browning and Horrocks watch the crossing*
3 *3/504th cross river at 1500 under cover of smoke-screen and gunfire*
4 *Irish Guards tanks*

providing gunfire support
5 *2/504th Parachute Infantry attacks Hunner Park at 1500*
6 *Grenadier Guards group clears the Valkhof and crosses bridge, 1800–1900*
7 *Grenadier Guards group, 2000*

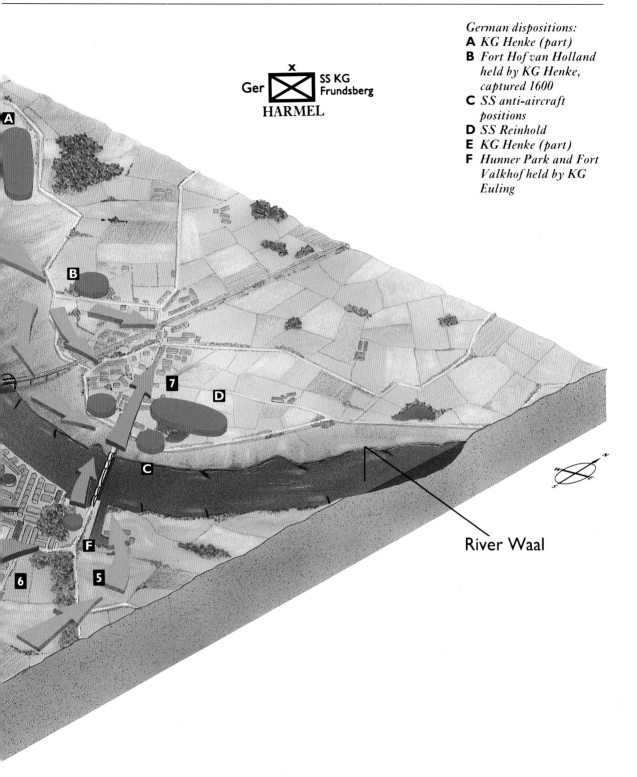

German dispositions:
A *KG Henke (part)*
B *Fort Hof van Holland held by KG Henke, captured 1600*
C *SS anti-aircraft positions*
D *SS Reinhold*
E *KG Henke (part)*
F *Hunner Park and Fort Valkhof held by KG Euling*

Ger ⊠ SS KG Frundsberg
HARMEL

River Waal

THE RIVER CROSSING AT NIJMEGEN

1500–2000 20 Sept 1944, as seen from the Groesbeek Heights

that relief of the bridge by Guards Armoured was now critical. The German bombardment continued, blasting down the buildings still held by the British and using flamethrowers to clear them from the rubble. At noon Frost himself was badly wounded by a mortar blast, and Major Gough took over command of the remaining troops. Almost out of ammunition, with wounded crowded into cellars, the British held on to their shrinking perimeter. Shortly after 1800 four PzKpfw VI Tiger tanks at last crashed their way across Arnhem bridge from north to south, but nothing else could follow them. At 2100 Gough negotiated a truce enabling the Germans to collect over 200 wounded of both sides from the cellars, including Frost who became a prisoner.

Much farther south, the British flanking operations remained painfully slow. In a last effort by XII Corps, 15th Division forced the line of the Wilhelmina Canal at Best, but still the village itself remained in German hands. VIII Corps began moving 69th Brigade of 50th Division northward to reinforce 101st Airborne, while 11th Armoured Division made some progress towards Helmond. With the German flanks growing stronger, these attacks across country stood little chance.

At Oosterbeek, far from expecting to crush 1st British Airborne, Model put Kampfgruppe 'von Tettau' under II SS Panzer Corps in order to check an expected breakout by Urquhart's troops. More German reinforcements continued to arrive, and XII SS Corps was expected with the new 180th Infantry Division and 190th Infantry Division within a week. In keeping with German doctrine rather than expecting any chance of success, Bittrich also ordered Harmel to counter-attack and retake Nijmegen next morning.

With only three battalions of the 'Frundsberg' between Nijmegen and Arnhem, it seemed that nothing could stop the Allies reaching Arnhem bridge that night. But on the other side Adair's Guards Armoured, fought to a standstill, would not advance at night into the *polder* of the 'island' without infantry, and Horrocks let them halt.

Meanwhile, far away from the battlefield, SHAEF Headquarters completed its move from Granville to Versailles, just west of Paris, drastically improving its communications. After four days, it was becoming clear to the senior Allied commanders that the original 'Market-Garden' plan had failed, and that the war against Germany was by no means over yet. The first hint of a change in attitude

◀ *Troops of 1st British Airborne with Sten submachine-guns, dug in to defend the Oosterbeek pocket beside their jeeps, late on Monday 18 September. Note that one is a signaller, still wearing his earphones and using the 22 radio set in the jeep beside him. This picture gives a good impression of the limited view from ground level of both sides when fighting in the pocket. (IWM photograph BU1143)*

▶ *Above right: On the other side of the Oosterbeek pocket, German infantry dug in among the trees. From their general appearance, these troops seem to be from one of the*

came when Montgomery at 21st Army Group Headquarters received a message from Eisenhower denying that SHAEF had ever intended a broad front advance and reaffirming priority for the northern thrust. With 'Market-Garden' a failure and both sides temporarily locked in an exhausted stalemate, the whole nature of the Battle of Arnhem was about to change.

various improvised formations which made up Kampfgruppe 'Von Tettau'. (IWM photograph MH3956)

▶ *A British casualty, with a leg wound, being carried by stretcher-bearers into one of the hotels or large houses used by 1st British Airborne as Main Dressing Stations. Later in the battle conditions became very overcrowded, and despite Red Cross markings it was almost impossible, among the houses and trees of Oosterbeek, for both sides to avoid firing at these positions before they were finally passed to German control. (IWM photograph BU1158)*

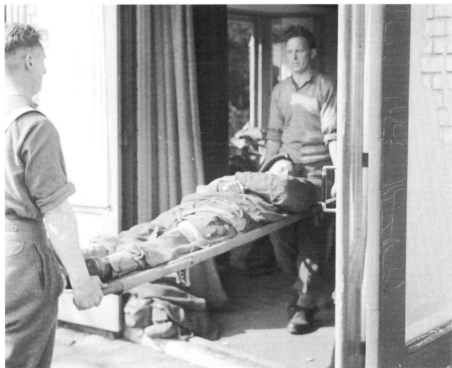

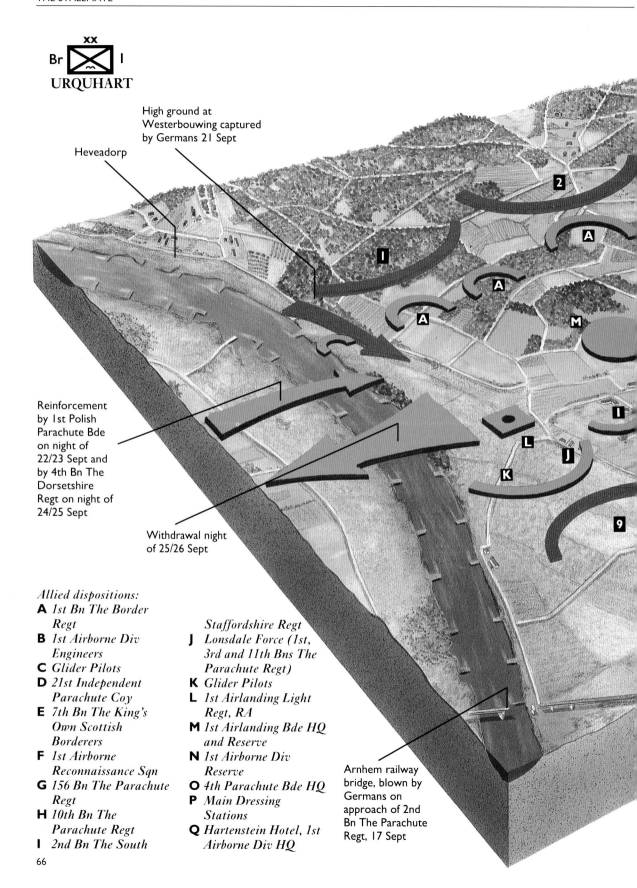

Br ⊠ I **URQUHART**

High ground at Westerbouwing captured by Germans 21 Sept

Heveadorp

Reinforcement by 1st Polish Parachute Bde on night of 22/23 Sept and by 4th Bn The Dorsetshire Regt on night of 24/25 Sept

Withdrawal night of 25/26 Sept

Arnhem railway bridge, blown by Germans on approach of 2nd Bn The Parachute Regt, 17 Sept

Allied dispositions:
A *1st Bn The Border Regt*
B *1st Airborne Div Engineers*
C *Glider Pilots*
D *21st Independent Parachute Coy*
E *7th Bn The King's Own Scottish Borderers*
F *1st Airborne Reconnaissance Sqn*
G *156 Bn The Parachute Regt*
H *10th Bn The Parachute Regt*
I *2nd Bn The South Staffordshire Regt*
J *Lonsdale Force (1st, 3rd and 11th Bns The Parachute Regt)*
K *Glider Pilots*
L *1st Airlanding Light Regt, RA*
M *1st Airlanding Bde HQ and Reserve*
N *1st Airborne Div Reserve*
O *4th Parachute Bde HQ*
P *Main Dressing Stations*
Q *Hartenstein Hotel, 1st Airborne Div HQ*

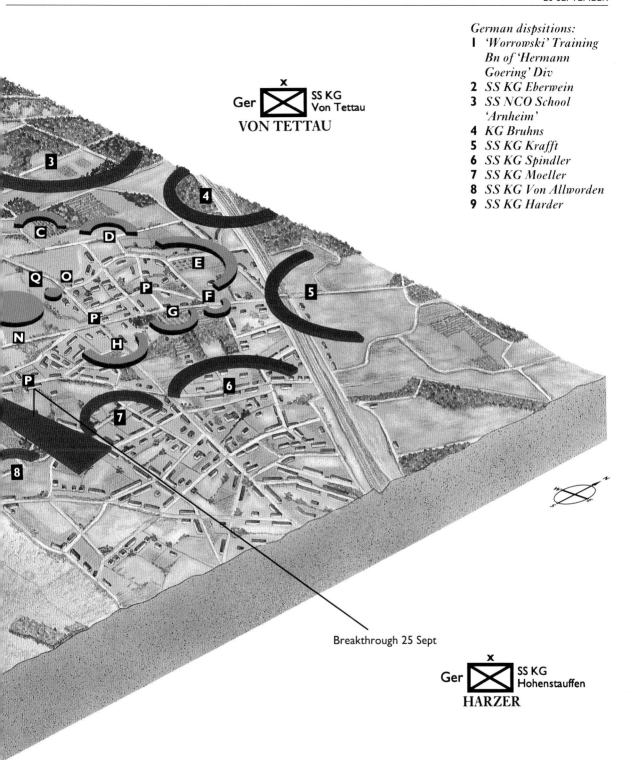

German dispsitions:
1 'Worrowski' Training Bn of 'Hermann Goering' Div
2 SS KG Eberwein
3 SS NCO School 'Arnheim'
4 KG Bruhns
5 SS KG Krafft
6 SS KG Spindler
7 SS KG Moeller
8 SS KG Von Allworden
9 SS KG Harder

Ger [X] SS KG Von Tettau
VON TETTAU

Breakthrough 25 Sept

Ger [X] SS KG Hohenstauffen
HARZER

1ST AIRBORNE DIVISION PERIMETER, OOSTERBEEK

20–26 Sept 1944, as seen from the direction of Arnhem Bridge

THE NEW ALLIED PLAN, 21 TO 22 SEPTEMBER

The fog and rain continued into Thursday (D plus 4), which was bitingly cold. As dawn arrived, Generalfeldmarschall Model at Army Group B issued fresh orders. Corps 'Feldt' was to hold its position. It had spent itself in the attack over the Groesbeek heights, and with Nijmegen bridge now in Allied hands there was little that it could do. Model placed all troops as far south as Elst under II SS Panzer Corps, which was to wipe out the British at Arnhem while containing any drive north of Nijmegen. Student's First Parachute Army was to organize a coordinated pincer attack by LXXXVIII Corps and LXXXVI Corps against Hell's Highway for next day.

At Arnhem bridge, the last fight began at about 0900, as Gough and his men tried to break out northwards against SS-Kampfgruppe 'Knaust'. There was no formal surrender or end to the fighting. In small groups, the British either ran out of ammunition or were overwhelmed. Some refused to give up or fought on with knives, and the last shots were not fired at Arnhem bridge for another two days. But at 1200, SS-Kampfgruppe 'Knaust' at last crossed Arnhem bridge. Frost's men had fought for 88 hours without relief, the last twelve of them without food or water.

In the Oosterbeek pocket, Urquhart re-organized his defence, placing Hicks in charge of

the western face against Kampfgruppe 'von Tettau', and Hackett in charge of the eastern face against SS-Kampfgruppe 'Hohenstauffen'. At 0900 an attack by Kampfgruppe 'von Tettau' drove 1st Battalion of the Border Regiment back off the Westerbouwing hill (30m high), the crucial high ground that overlooked the Heveadorp ferry, and away from the ferry itself, which was destroyed in the fighting. From the Westerbouwing, German fire could dominate any attempted river crossing. In their confusion and exhaustion, neither side had appreciated the vital significance of this ground. Kampfgruppe 'von Tettau' pushed Hick's troops back about 800m during the day, but Model's orders to eliminate the British pocket could not be carried out with the available forces. Instead, the Germans set up loudspeakers to play music to the British, along with invitations to surrender, while the sniping and mortaring continued.

At Nijmegen, the way across the two bridges was finally cleared of German snipers by 1000. Two hours later, while the Grenadiers recovered, the

◄ *Arnhem bridge, taken by a German photographer from the north side of the ramp looking south, shortly after the last stand of Frost's men, Thursday 21 September. The burnt out German pillbox can be seen to the right of the bridge, together with the rubble of buildings destroyed in the fighting. The vehicles wrecked in 9th SS Reconnaissance Battalion's attack have been cleared away to the left and the bridge is now open. (IWM photograph HU2127)*

Irish Guards led off northwards with the Welsh Guards following. The attack started just as SS-Kampfgruppe 'Knaust' was crossing Arnhem bridge. Short of ammunition, artillery and air cover, the tanks of the Guards Armoured pushed up the exposed causeway road as far as Elst, and halted in the face of German fire. By 1600, SS-Kampfgruppe 'Knaust' had reached Elst from Arnhem to establish a firm block.

Meanwhile, 43rd Division, which was still waiting for its last brigade to get through from Eindhoven, was busy clearing the remaining pockets of German resistance from Nijmegen. Horrocks ordered the division, under Major General G. I. Thomas, to take over the lead from the spent Guards Armoured, advance through Driel and link up with 1st British Airborne at Heveadorp. Relieved of much of the responsibility for Nijmegen, 82nd Airborne began a general attack late in the afternoon with 504th Parachute Infantry and 508th Parachute Infantry, which cleared Corps 'Feldt' off the Groesbeek heights before establishing a solid defence.

During the afternoon, 1st British Airborne established firm radio contact with XXX Corps through the Royal Artillery's 64th Medium Regiment. The distance from Nijmegen to Arnhem is only 17km (eleven miles), and through this link Urquart could call for fire support from the whole of XXX Corps' artillery, drastically reducing the German advantage north of the Lower Rhine. Without this fire support the Oosterbeek pocket could not have been held, and after the battle Urquhart tried unsuccessfully to have 64th Medium Regiment awarded British Airborne insignia. In response to this stiffening resistance, Model ordered specialist troops and equipment for street fighting to be flown into Deelen by Junkers Ju 52 transport aircraft, and was promised 506th Heavy Tank Battalion, freshly equipped with 45 of the formidable PzKpfw VIB King Tiger tanks, from eastern Germany.

Back in England, 1st Polish Parachute Brigade's three infantry battalions took off at 1400, flying on the northern route. Of its 114 Dakotas, 41 turned back in the bad weather (including virtually the whole of 1st Battalion) and three landed in Brussels. Over Driel more than 100 Luftwaffe fighters were

◀ *Paratroops of 1st Polish Parachute Brigade at last preparing to take off on Thursday 21 September. This picture gives an unusually good view of the manner in which British-style equipment was fitted over the Denison smock before donning the parachute harness. The soldier on the right is rearranging his face veil before fitting his helmet.*

◄ *Paratroopers of 82nd Airborne Division watch as Cromwell tanks of the Guards Armoured Division, probably from 2nd (Armoured Reconnaissance) Battalion of the Welsh Guards, move across Nijmegen bridge northward towards Arnhem on the morning of Thursday 21 September. The low, flat ground of the 'island' can be seen in the distance on the right. (IWM photograph B10172)*

waiting for the Poles, of which 25 broke through and together with anti-aircraft fire claimed thirteen more Dakotas. At 1700, Major-General Sosabowski landed at Driel with 750 men and no heavy equipment, which had been lost in the gliders two days before.

To the Germans, the Polish landing, coinciding with the move south to Elst by SS-Kampfgruppe 'Knaust' to confront the Guards Armoured, appeared as an attempt to outflank them and capture Arnhem bridge once more from the south. Obersturmbahnführer Harzer rapidly organized 2,500 sailors, airmen, coastal defence troops, Dutch SS police and German infantry as a blocking force (known as 'Sperrverband Harzer') between the Poles and the bridge, west of the Nijmegen road. Flying resupply after the Poles, 115 transport aircraft of RAF 38 Group were intercepted by ten Fw 190s which broke through the fighter screen again. Some 23 resupply aircraft were shot down and 38 damaged by fighters or flak, and only 41 out of 300

A Sherman V tank of the Guards Armoured Division. This tank, 'Monck', is the command tank of Lieutenant Colonel R. F. S. Gooch, MC, 1st (Armoured) Battalion, Coldstream Guards, identifiable from the 'All Seeing Eye' formation sign of the Guards Division, the regimental number '52', and the HQ squadron diamond, all on the stowage box fitted to the nose of the tank, and the regimental flag displayed. The hull machine-gun has been removed to accommodate an extra radio operator, and there is an extra aerial fitted at the right hull position.

▲ *500ft (160 metres) above Driel at 1700 on Thursday 21 September, the leading paratroopers of 1st Polish Parachute Brigade prepare to leave the jump door of their C-47 Dakota. The Dakota had only one jump door, which some pilots preferred to leave open during the flight. It was known for the leading paratrooper of the 'stick' of fifteen men to become wedged in the door if the pilot manoeuvred suddenly to avoid enemy fire. After the jump signal was given, the actual moment of jumping was often left to the 'stick' leader, who would watch for obstacles.*

tons got through to the British at Oosterbeek. After nightfall, the Poles began planning to cross the Lower Rhine, but no boats arrived from XXX Corps before dawn.

North of Eindhoven, 101st Airborne continued to push the Germans back on either side of Hell's Highway in a series of limited attacks supported by British armour. The drives by VIII Corps and XII Corps, which had fought their way across country roughly level with the line of the Wilhelmina Canal, had come virtually to a halt. Lieutenant General Dempsey began to move Second Army Headquarters to St Oedenrode, and Field Marshal Montgomery established 21st Army Group Tactical Headquarters just south of Eindhoven to be in closer touch with the battle.

In response to General Eisenhower's earlier message, Montgomery sent a signal to SHAEF demanding that Eisenhower make good his commitment to the northern thrust by halting Patton's Third US Army and placing Hodges' First US Army at least under some form of British control. On the same day, Patton arrived at Versailles with Bradley's blessing, demanding more troops for his thrust across the Rhine. Eisenhower's response was to summon a major conference of his Army Group and Army commanders – the first since before the D-Day landings on 6 June – for the next day.

Friday 22 September (D plus 5) was very misty, and there were no resupply flights from England, but the weather was beginning to lift. At 0900 General Student's attack on Hell's Highway began with Kampfgruppe 'Huber' (part of 59th Infantry Divison) from the west and Kampfgruppe 'Walther' (now mainly 107th Panzer Brigade) from the east, breaking through to cut the largely undefended section of road between Uden and Grave. This also split 69th Brigade of British 50th Division, which was moving up to cover the gap between 101st Airborne and 82nd Airborne. In response, 101st Airborne, now under XXX Corps with its long familiarity with air support procedures, obtained 119 rocket-firing Typhoon sorties from RAF 83 Group along Hell's Highway during the day.

Not far away over Kleve, completely divorced from the Arnhem battle, 9th Air Force fighters dominated the skies, while 8th Air Force and Bomber Command, whose bombers might have influenced the battle considerably, flew raids against German cities. Only at Arnhem and Nijmegen did the Germans continue to enjoy air superiority. Lieutenant General Dempsey's chief of staff, attempting to reach Horrocks at Nijmegen by aircraft, was shot down but survived.

Major General Taylor received some warning of the German pincer attack through the PAN, and rushed 150 men of 506th Parachute Infantry to Uden by 1100, only minutes before the German tanks arrived. A limited attack north-west by 501st and 502nd Parachute Infantry had to be abandoned as Kampfgruppe 'Huber' reached Veghel by 1400, putting the bridge under fire, and in the course of the fighting Colonel John H. Michaelis, commanding 501st Parachute Infantry, was seriously wounded. Brigadier General Anthony McAuliffe, the division's artillery commander, began with 2/501st Parachute Infantry defending Veghel and finished with eight battalions as American and British reinforcements arrived. Horrocks was forced to turn the whole of 32nd Guards Brigade (the Grenadiers and Coldstream) around to drive back south down Hell's Highway from Grave to Uden, clearing the road of Germans. For a crucial day, supplies and equipment, above all river crossing equipment, could not travel beyond Veghel.

The renewed attempt by XXX Corps to reach 1st British Airborne began shortly after dawn with orders from Horrocks to take all risks. 43rd Divison attacked north from Nijmegen, with 214th Brigade moving towards Driel, while 129th Brigade and the Irish Guards Group attacked at Elst. On the exposed 'island' movement within sight of the enemy was almost impossible for either side, and unsupported vehicles were open targets. But at 0830 a few armoured cars of the Household Cavalry found a route through to the Poles at Driel. Strictly, this completed the link between XXX Corps and 1st British Airborne, four days and eighteen hours since the start of 'Market-Garden'. That afternoon Lieutenant Colonel Mackenzie crossed the Lower Rhine and used the Households' radios to send a long signal to Horrocks and Browning before driving off to Nijmegen. By late afternoon a single infantry battalion, 5th Battalion of the Duke of Cornwall's Light Infantry with some tanks, had reached the Poles.

At 2100 Sosabowski, acting on Horrocks' orders, attempted a river crossing towards Heveadorp with four rubber boats, all that were available. Under intense German fire, about 50 Poles crossed, of whom 35 survived to join the Border Regiment. A plan for 5th Battalion of the Duke of Cornwall's Light Infantry to follow them later that night was called off as no further boats or DUKW amphibious craft had arrived. German attacks continued all around the Oosterbeek pocket, and at 2144 Urquhart signalled Browning that relief within 24 hours was vital. Bittrich meanwhile conferred with Harzer and von Tettau to plan the final destruction of 1st British Airborne next day.

▶ *The PAN (Dutch) resistance made a major contribution to 'Market-Garden', although they were shot by the Germans if caught fighting on the Allied side. Here two PAN men, wearing identifying orange armbands, pass information to officers on the Intelligence staff of 50th (Northumbrian) Division near Valkenswaard on Monday 25 September (note the 'Tyne-Tees' shoulder flash of the two British officers). Failure to make proper use of PAN information contributed to 1st British Airborne Division's problems at Arnhem. (IWM photograph B10313)*

While the fighting raged all day from Veghel to Oosterbeek, Eisenhower's Army Group and Army commanders assembled at Versailles. Even for this vital meeting, Montgomery stuck to his custom and sent Major General de Guingand to represent him, reportedly because he did not trust himself to speak to the American generals. This meeeting began to repair the mistakes in the original 'Market-Garden' plan, as Eisenhower asserted the authority that had drifted for the last month. Instead of individual actions against a defeated enemy, Eisenhower now insisted on a coordinated advance to the Rhine by all his Armies, stressing the importance of First Canadian Army's attack to clear the Scheldt and open Antwerp now that the war was going to last beyond September. Bradley was instructed to halt Patton (the formal order to Third US Army was issued next day), while First US Army was ordered to swing northwards towards Aachen, sending XIX Corps under Major General Charles H. Corlett (temporarily reduced by Bradley to two divisions) northwards to cooperate with British VIII Corps. In return, Second British Army would change its axis of advance, with VIII Corps leading north-east across country towards Venlo and Kleve, instead of XXX Corps heading north past Arnhem. Although First US Army remained under Bradley, Montgomery was allowed direct communication with it.

That afternoon Montgomery visited 3rd Division at Weert, the first of a series of visits to explain the new plan throughout Second British Army. Although a bridgehead at Arnhem might be useful, and there were humanitarian reasons for saving 1st British Airborne, from this point XXX Corps' efforts north of Nijmegen became a secondary operation, and any idea of an advance past Arnhem was given up. It says much for Montgomery's state of mind that he seems to have believed that this new plan was feasible, and that Lieutenant General O'Connor might yet rescue his battle for him.

Next day, Lieutenant General Dempsey placed 101st Airborne under VIII Corps, while 50th Division was reinforced by 131st Brigade of 7th Armoured from XII Corps, and – together with the Royal Netherlands Brigade 'Prinses Irene' – took over Nijmegen from 43rd Division. VIII Corps now had to fight on two fronts: while 101st Airborne and 50th Division defended against attacks from the west and north-west, 3rd Division and 11th Armoured Division were to drive north-east to the Rhine, keeping step with US XIX Corps. Horrocks' XXX Corps was left with the troops north of Grave – 43rd Division, 82nd Airborne and the fragmented Guards Armoured – while I Airborne Corps continued to command the survivors of 1st British Airborne. After meetings between Montgomery, Dempsey, their Army Corps and divisional commanders, Second British Army signalled I Airborne Corps at 2020 that it had permission to withdraw 1st British Airborne if necessary, just over 24 hours after Urquhart's appeal.

▲ *Major General 'Roy' Urquhart on the back lawn of his headquarters at the Hartenstein Hotel, Friday 22 September, with 1st British Airborne Division's pennon beside him. Except for his red beret and rank badges, Urquhart is dressed in the regulation battledress uniform for all British officers. Previously a brigadier in the 51st (Highland) Division, he was promoted to lead 1st British Airborne in January 1944 without previous airborne experience. Despite his very orthodox approach, Urquhart was regarded by many in the division as an outstanding leader. (IWM photograph BU1136)*

THE END AT ARNHEM, 23 TO 26 SEPTEMBER

Saturday 23 September (D plus 6) produced the first good weather since the start of 'Market-Garden', despite the morning fog and the rain that night, and 2nd Tactical Air Force was heavily active over Oosterbeek. With artillery and air support, 1st British Airborne held on to its foxholes and houses, and once more Harzer and von Tettau could not break through the perimeter. In the afternoon, an angry Model visited II SS Panzer Corps Headquarters and gave Bittrich 24 more hours to wipe 1st British Airborne out. Model also changed Army Group B's command structure, placing all forces west of the 'Market-Garden' salient under Fifteenth Army, and all those to the east under First Parachute Army, at last relieving Armed Forces Command Netherlands and Wehrkreiss VI of their fighting responsibilities. So far, Model's defensive scheme had largely succeeded, stopping 'Market--Garden' only two-thirds of the way to its objective on the Zuider Zee. Now, in the classic manner of German counterstrokes on the Eastern Front, he planned to destroy both I Airborne Corps and XXX Corps north of Nijmegen and regain the line of the Waal.

Farther south, the Germans renewed their attacks against Veghel in the morning with 6th Parachute Regiment (now part of Kampfgruppe 'Chill') from the west and Kampfgruppe 'Walther' from the east, but they were both driven off by noon. Three hours later, 506th Parachute Infantry with British armour linked with 32nd Guards Brigade at Uden, reopening Hell's Highway.

At 1300, the delayed last wave of airborne reinforcements took off from England in the largest 'Market-Garden' airlift since its first day. Escorted by fighters of 8th Air Force, 654 troop carriers and 490 gliders flew on the northern route almost without incident to land at 1500. 82nd Airborne received 3,385 troops in 428 gliders, mainly the delayed 325th Glider Infantry Regiment, which

A captain in the Royal Netherlands Brigade 'Prinses Irene', wearing British battledress and equipment with Dutch rank badges, including brigade shoulder flash, 'Lion' cap badge and Dutch national 'Lion and Netherlands' sleeve badge.

▲ *Major General Sosabowski, in Denison smock and paratrooper's uniform, at his head-quarters in the woods east of Driel with Major General G. I. Thomas commanding 43rd (Wessex) Division, probably on Saturday 23 September. Thomas is wearing an unusual uniform of pre-war style boots, puttees and breeches with a battle-dress blouse worn over a sleeveless sweater and motoring goggles around his general's cap. With a reputation for offering unwelcome advice, Thomas did not get on well with Sosabowski and was heavily criticized for his division's slowness during 'Market-Garden'.*

dropped at Oude Keent, a disused airfield just outside Grave which I Airborne Corps planned to use for resupply. The battalion then marched northwards to join its brigade, which had been placed under 130th Brigade of 43rd Division by Horrocks. At Driel, 41 USAAF Dakotas dropped supplies and equipment to Sosabowski, who was increasingly ready to show his disgust with his treatment and that of his brigade by the British.

On the 'island', XXX Corps' advance against SS-Kampfgruppe 'Frundsberg' made little prog-ress, delayed until supplies and equipment could reach it while Hell's Highway was cleared farther south. Late in the morning Lieutenant Colonel Mackenzie finally reached Browning at I Airborne Corps Headquarters. Browning gave Mackenzie a message of greeting to take back to Urquhart, but other than expressing his anger with 43rd Division's slow progress he had nothing to offer. That afternoon 130th Brigade with more river crossing equipment linked up with the Poles at Driel, and after nightfall Sosabowksi sent 200 men of his 1st Battalion across the Lower Rhine in assault boats to join 1st British Airborne. Next morning Mackenzie also recrossed the Lower Rhine to rejoin his division.

On Sunday 24 September (D plus 7) the weather remained reasonable after some morning fog, and 2nd Tactical Air Force flew 22 close air support sorties for 1st British Airborne from mid-afternoon, despite problems in identifying targets in the shrinking Oosterbeek pocket. Through XXX Corps artillery support and its own fighting qualities, 1st British Airborne continued to hold the perimeter, although Brigadier Hackett was wounded by a shellburst that morning. Urquhart's men were now threatened with the same fate that had overwhelmed Frost, a collapse from exhaustion and lack of ammunition. At 1500 a medical truce came into force, carefully negotiated between 1st British Airborne and II SS Panzer Corps, which allowed the transfer of 700 wounded to the Germans, followed by 500 more next day. This left Urquhart with about 1,800 troops organized in small groups to defend the pocket.

Both sides at Arnhem had now been fighting for a week without rest, almost without sleep, and a single fresh formation might swing the battle. This

should have arrived four days before. 101st Airborne received 907th Glider Field Artillery Battalion and the last of 327th Glider Infantry. The seaborne tails of both divisions also arrived from England through the Normandy beaches, com-pleting their deployment.

1st Battalion of 1st Polish Parachute Brigade, which had turned back on Thursday 21 September,

▲ *Two British paratroops, one of them wearing the sleeveless 'jump jacket', fit a Mark 1 Weapons Container underneath an aircraft before take-off in England. Fitted with its own parachute, this container was used to carry a variety of stores and equipment. Other stores were dropped directly from the open doors of the cargo aircraft. (IWM photograph H37727)*

▼ *Troops of 1st Airborne Division in the grounds of the Hartenstein Hotel displaying yellow parachutes as a guide to Allied aircraft dropping supplies, probably on Saturday 23 September. As this picture shows, even when the Allied pilots were aware of the intended supply drop zones, picking them out from among the trees and houses was extremely difficult. (IWM photograph BU1119)*

◀ Top: German infantry in the Oosterbeek pocket, late in the fighting. The mixture of uniforms worn and weapons carried by these men tells its own story. The German ability to assemble improvised forces at short notice was much admired by the Allies, but although these could be strong in defence, they had great difficulty making coordinated attacks. (IWM photograph HU2126)

◀ Men of the Glider Pilot Regiment, carrying Sten submachine-guns and pistols, fight their way through the rubble of a building in Oosterbeek, Saturday 23 September. The 1,200 men of the Gilder Pilot Regiment at Arhem formed two 'Wings', each the equivalent of a battalion, and played a major part in the defence of the perimeter. (IWM photograph BU1121)

▲ A British ammunition truck explodes, scattering incendiaries on to the road, having been hit by fire from Parachute Battalion 'Jungwirth' near Koevering on 'Hell's Highway', on the evening of Sunday 24 September. Much of the road at this point was lined with trees, making ambush easier for the Germans. (IWM photograph B10124A)

arrived on the German side in the form of the King Tigers of 506th Heavy Tank Battalion, of which two companies (30 tanks) were sent to the 'Frundsberg' near Elst and one company to the east side of the Oosterbeek pocket. Even before these tanks arrived, XXX Corps had made only slow progress north of Nijmegen against the German defence. The only success that day was the capture of Bemmel by 69th Brigade and the Welsh Guards.

At 0930 Horrocks, together with Thomas and Sosabowski, surveyed the far side of the Lower Rhine from the steeple of Driel church. Thomas came away believing that Horrocks had issued orders for the withdrawal of 1st British Airborne that night, and began planning a crossing to seize the Westerbouwing and help Urquhart. Horrocks, who later denied he had issued these orders, then went to Second British Army Headquarters to consult Dempsey. Who actually gave the order to withdraw from Arnhem cannot be established, but Montgomery notified London of the decision, and the forthcoming thrust north-east by VIII Corps, that evening. As news of the planned withdrawal spread there was a late flurry of activity from the airborne commanders. First Allied Airborne Army

◀ *Officers of 1st Polish Parchute Brigade, 1st Airborne Division and 43rd Division at Sosabowksi's headquarters east of Driel, probably Saturday 23 September, planning the river crossing by 4th Battalion of the Dorsetshire Regiment. Note the 'Wessex Wyvern' divisional patch of the Dorsets' officer left, and that like many officers Sosabowski wears no rank or identifying badges on his Denison smock. This often makes precise identification of airborne troops from photographs extremely difficult.*

tried to arrange for 8th Air Force fighters to drop belly tanks full of supplies to 1st British Airborne, while Browning now wanted 52nd (Lowland) Division flown in, a suggestion vetoed by Dempsey and Montgomery.

In response to Generalfeldmarschall von Rundstedt's suggestion that all German troops in Holland should fall back to the Maas in the face of Second British Army's offensive, Hitler demanded instead a renewed offensive at Nijmegen and Veghel. Model took full advantage of this by requesting even more reinforcements, including the full strength 363rd Volksgrenadier Division, which could not arrive until after the battle.

The renewed attack on Hell's Highway by Kampfgruppe 'Chill' began shortly after dawn, looking for weak spots in 101st Airborne's line. Most of the Germans were heavily repulsed, but as dusk fell the weak Parachute Battalion 'Jungwirth', reinforced by a company of Jagdpanthers of 559th Assault Battalion, cut the road once again at Koevering, just south of Veghel. Horrocks at St Oedenrode with Dempsey found that he was cut off from XXX Corps HQ for the day. No attack took place from KG 'Walther', which was finally forced to retreat by 11th Armoured Division's capture of Deurne, east of Helmond, opening the way for VIII Corps' advance. Nevertheless, with Hell's Highway closed to supply traffic once more, Dempsey ordered O'Connor to hold in place.

▶ *Wounded survivors of 1st British Airborne captured by the Germans as they occupied the Oosterbeek pocket on Tuesday 26 September. One of these men appears to have been given a German greatcoat to wear. As in virtually all battles, there were incidents on both sides at Arnhem of surrendering soldiers being shot. But, aware of the reputation of the Waffen-SS for brutality, the wounded soldiers were surprised at how well they were treated by the Germans. (IWM photograph HU2131)*

At 0200 on Monday 25 September (D plus 8), 43rd Division made its crossing of the Lower Rhine to help 1st British Airborne in darkness, heavy rain and strong winds. But there were boats and DUKW amphibious craft only for two companies, or 350 men, of 4th Battalion of the Dorsetshire Regiment, of whom 315 reached the far bank to be pinned down at once by German fire. Kampfgruppe 'von Tettau' took 140 prisoners including the battalion commander, and although the Dorsets briefly held part of the Westerbouwing they achieved little else. At 0808 Urquhart signalled Thomas that the evacuation, codenamed Operation 'Berlin', must take place that night. As if to emphasize the point, SS-Kampfgruppe 'von Allworden' with the new

King Tigers of 506th Heavy Tank Battalion attacked that afternoon from the east, driving deep into Urquhart's position and threatening to encircle 1st British Airborne. Artillery and 81 close-support sorties from 2nd Tactical Air Force helped the British troops hold out for another day.

During the morning, as XXX Corps finally secured Elst as well as Boxmeer, Horrocks and Browning met at I Airborne Corps Headquarters to discuss 'Berlin', while Montgomery and Dempsey met at Eindhoven. With so many Germans concentrated at Oosterbeek, the Household Cavalry patrols revealed that the Lower Rhine west of Arnhem was almost undefended, and Horrocks briefly considered making another crossing. Instead,

43rd Division mounted a simulated crossing at Renkum, 6km (four miles) west of Oosterbeek, that night to help the withdrawal.

With assistance from British 50th Division and 7th Armoured, 506th and 502nd Parachute Infantry moved against Hoevering during the day, and at nightfall the surrounded Germans abandoned their position, having mined the road first. This was LXXXVIII Corps' last effort, and next day 101st Airborne cleared the mines and re-opened Hell's Highway for good.

Farther east, VIII Corps drove forward against the retreating Kampfgruppe 'Walther' and 180th Infantry Division. By nightfall, 11th Armoured had reached the Maas at Boxmeer, linking up with XXX Corps. But with only two divisions attacking north-eastward, O'Connor was now completely over-extended. On the Willems Canal line, 3rd Division, already holding 35km (22 miles) of front, was faced with the prospect of holding 51km (32 miles) next day. It was only saved by the arrival of 7th US Armored Division, newly returned to Corlett's US XIX Corps, which came into line beside it.

At 2100 on the Lower Rhine 'Berlin' began with a sustained bombardment by 43rd Division and XXX Corps artillery that lasted eleven hours. At 2140 two companies of Royal Canadian Engineers with 21 stormboats (each holding fourteen men) and two Royal Engineer companies with sixteen assault boats started to cross the river. Leaving behind their wounded with some volunteers, 1st British Airborne started to withdraw in the pouring rain through a gap barely 700m wide to the river bank. The

Germans continued heavy mortaring and took 170 prisoners, but there was no attempt to rush the British troops, and by 0130 the withdrawal north of the Hartenstein Hotel was complete. At 0200 the division's ammunition was blown up and its guns disabled, and at first light the ferrying ended. The survivors of 1st British Airborne marched from

A sergeant of 508th Parachute Infantry, 82nd Airborne Division, wearing the new M1943 field uniform, given to the Airborne troops after Normandy to replace the light khaki M1942 paratrooper's uniform. Note the 'All American' divisional sign on one sleeve and the American flag on the other. He wears jump boots and an M1C paratrooper's helmet, and carries an M3 'Grease Gun' submachine-gun. The AL-141 Signal Panel (white on one side, orange on the other) was used to mark drop and landing zones.

◀ *Top: A German officer (with cap) identified as Brigadeführer Heinz Harmel, accompanied by some formidable-looking members of his SS-Kampfgruppe 'Frunds-berg', talks to a Polish prisoner, probably in Arnhem on Tuesday 26 September. The Pole may be acting as an interpreter for the other prisoners visible in the building behind them. (IWM photograph HU2133)*

◀ *Survivors of 1st British Airborne recover-ing from Operation 'Berlin' in the grounds of the Missionary College in Nijmegen on Tuesday 26 September. Between them these privates and NCOs represent almost every regiment of 1st British Airborne which fought at Arnhem, but most are from 1st Battalion of the Border Regiment. (IWM photograph HU3722).*

Driel to Nijmegen, where their divisional seaborne tail was waiting with clean uniforms and equipment. By 1400 the Germans had occupied the remains of the Oosterbeek pocket, capturing the wounded troops who could not be moved.

With the end of 'Berlin' at 0550 on Tuesday 26 September (D plus 9), 'Market-Garden' also ended. Since the start of the operation, First Allied Airborne Army had dispatched 4,852 troop-carrying aircraft successfully to their destinations, of which 1,293 delivered paratroops, 2,277 gliders, and 1,282 resupply. Altogether 164 aircraft and 132 gliders were lost. USAAF IX Troop Carrier Command suffered 454 casualties, RAF 38 and 46 Groups a further 294 casualties. Some 39,620 troops were delivered by air to their targets (21,074 by parachute and 18,546 by glider) with 4,595 tons of stores. However, only 7.4 per cent of the stores intended for 1st British Airborne actually reached it.

A further 6,172 aircraft sorties were flown in support of 'Market-Garden', more than half of them by 8th Air Force, for the loss of 125 aircraft. It is significant that 2nd Tactical Air Force flew only 534 of these sorties, and 9th Air Force 209 sorties. Browning complained that 2nd Tactical Air Force had turned down 46 out of 95 requests for air support from I Airborne Corps Headquarters, chiefly on grounds of poor target identification. The Allied airforces claimed 160 enemy aircraft shot down, and rescued 205 men from the North Sea during the operation.

At Arnhem itself, 10,300 men of 1st British Airborne Division and 1st Polish Parachute Brigade landed from the air. Some 2,587 men escaped across the Rhine in Operation 'Berlin' (1,741 of 1st British Airborne, 422 of the Glider Pilot Regiment, 160 Poles and 75 from the Dorsetshire Regiment), and 240 more returned later with the aid of the PAN. About 1,600 wounded were left behind in the Oosterbeek pocket, together with 204 medical officers and chaplains who volunteered to stay. The Germans claimed 6,450 prisoners taken, wounded or not, and 1st British Airborne therefore lost about 1,300 killed. The highest proportionate losses were suffered by the Glider Pilot Regiment and Major Gough's Reconnaissance Squadron, each with more than one in five men killed. Three out of nine battalion commanders of 1st Airborne Division were killed, four more were wounded and taken prisoner, together with two out of three brigade commanders. Five Victoria Crosses were won at Arnhem, four of them posthumous including one to a resupply aircraft pilot.

In the course of the battle, 1st Polish Parachute Brigade lost 378 casualties. The two American airborne divisions lost 3,664 men together: 1,432 from 82nd Airborne, 2,110 from 101st Airborne and 122 glider pilots. One American battalion commander was killed, another was badly wounded, a regimental commander was also wounded, and two posthumous Medals of Honor were won.

By its own estimate, the total losses for I Airborne Corps were 6,858 men. Second British Army's casualties for 'Market-Garden' alone are harder to calculate, but one estimate places them at 5,354 including 1,480 for XXX Corps, giving a total of 16,805 Allied casualties. German casualties, like their unit strengths, cannot be given accurately for this period of the war. Generalfeldmarschall Model estimated Army Group B casualties in 'Market-Garden' at 3,300, but other calculations place them as high as 2,000 dead and 6,000 wounded.

At 0200, as the last of his men were crossing the Lower Rhine, a soaked and exhausted Major General Urquhart reached I Airborne Corps Headquarters and demanded to see Lieutenant General Browning, who rose and dressed to see Urquhart for a brief conversation before directing him to bed. That evening Browning held a formal dinner party for Horrocks, Urquhart and Thomas, putting his chef to good use. Next morning, Wednesday 27 September, Urquhart went south to 21st Army Group Headquarters at Eindhoven to brief Dempsey and Montgomery himself on the battle.

In the 'Market-Garden' corridor, 21st Army Group was digging in. Its front, already 240km (150 miles) long on 16 September, had been extended by a long thin finger of territory stretching up Hell's Highway from Joe's Bridge to Driel, and from Boxmeer to Oss where 7th Armoured Division of XII Corps had finally linked with the Guards Armoured, adding another 200km (130 miles) to be defended. The fighting to hold this salient would continue, but the Battle of Arnhem was over.

◄ *A Sherman tank of the Guards Armoured Division pushes up past a knocked out PzKpfw IV, not far from Uden on Wednesday 27 September. The German tank may well be from 107th Panzer Brigade, which like all German formations at this date had a mixture of vehicles. Note the extra sections of track bolted to the front of the Sherman's hull to give it better armoured protection. (IWM photograph B10375)*

THE AFTERMATH OF THE BATTLE

The end of Operation 'Market-Garden' was no more tidy than its beginning. The new salient held by Second British Army threatened to cut off most of the German troops in western Holland once the attack to clear the Scheldt began, and on 27 September 712th Static Division of LXXXVIII Corps tried to escape through Grave, only to be repulsed by the Coldstream. Next morning two major Luftwaffe air attacks by more than 40 aircraft including Me 262 fighter-bombers damaged both bridges at Nijmegen. This was followed by a suicide attack that night on the bridges by twelve German frogmen, which closed them for 24 hours.

On 1 October Generalfeldmarschall Model began his counter-attack against XXX Corps on the 'island' with II SS Panzer Corps from the north, XII SS Corps from the west and II Parachute Corps from the east across the Groesbeek heights. In five days the German offensive over the open *polder* was heavily defeated by Allied firepower, and on 7 October II SS Panzer Corps gave up its attacks. On the same day USAAF and RAF bombing raids closed Arnhem bridge to traffic, and on 4 February 1945 the Germans themselves blew it into the Lower Rhine.

The survivors of 1st British Airborne returned to a heroes' welcome in Britain within a week of their evacuation from Arnhem, and 1st Polish Parachute Brigade joined them shortly afterwards. But the German threat to the new salient made it

◄ *Left to right, Lieutenant General Ritchie commanding XII Corps (smoking one of his famous cheroots), Lieutenant General O'Connor commanding VIII Corps, Major General D. A. H. Graham commanding 50th (Northumbrian) Division, Dempsey and Montgomery review the situation map at the end of 'Market-Garden' at Graham's divisional headquarters near Best, Thursday 28 September. Major General Verne commanding 7th Armoured Division was also present. Despite the smiles for the camera, Montgomery would recommend O'Connor's replacement that night. (IWM photograph B10388).*

A private of the Parachute Regiment, armed with a Mark II Sten submachine-gun and wearing a Denison smock over the Airborne version of battledress with the famous red (strictly maroon) beret and Parachute Regiment badge, a face veil worn around the neck as normal, and ammunition boots with anklets. The wounded man is a lieutenant of the Royal Army Medical Corps with a field dressing tied over his face. Note the lieutenant's glider badge and Fairbairn-Sykes fighting knife, strictly a breach of the convention which forbade medical staff carrying weapons.

impossible to withdraw the two American airborne divisions. On 5 October, 101st Airborne took over 43rd Division's position on the 'island', just in time to repell Model's last attack, made by 363rd Volksgrenadier Division. Over Brereton's protests, Montgomery convinced Eisenhower to let him keep 82nd Airborne in line until 13 November and 101st Airborne until 27 November. The two divisions took more casualties in this period than during 'Market-Garden' itself. Major General Taylor was slightly wounded, and Colonel Howard Johnson, commanding 501st Parachute Infantry, was killed.

The Battle of Antwerp to clear the Scheldt estuary began almost simultaneously with the end of 'Market-Garden'. It lasted until 28 November, when Antwerp was officially opened to cargo ships, and cost 21st Army Group 30,000 casualties. In response to the Dutch transport strike called to coincide with 'Market-Garden', the Germans halted all civilian transport in the country, and 18,000 Dutch civilians died in the 'hunger winter' that followed. Nevertheless, the PAN continued to help

Allied soldiers on the run in northern Holland. Brigadier Lathbury with 142 men escaped to safety in October, and Brigadier Hackett the following February.

The failure at Arnhem and the need to open the Scheldt condemned the troops of both 21st Army Group and Army Group B to a miserable winter fighting in the flat and flooded terrain of Holland. In the spring, Allied attention turned to crossing the Rhine into Germany rather than clearing Holland, and Arnhem was not finally liberated by British troops of First Canadian Army until 14 April 1945.

The OB West report on 'Market-Garden', produced in October 1944, gave the decision to spread the airborne landings over more than one day as the main reason for the Allied failure. A Luftwaffe analysis added that the airborne landings were spread too thinly and made too far from the Allied front line. General Student regarded the Allied airborne landings as an immense success and blamed the final failure to reach Arnhem on XXX Corps' slow progress. In this respect, General-

◀ *At the end of 'Market-Garden', an Intelligence officer of 1st Polish Parachute Brigade asks questions of his men while an officer of 1st British Airborne Division (with his back to the camera) listens. 1st British Airborne flew back to England on 30 September, followed by the Poles on 7 October, three days before Browning's after-action report on the battle was submitted.*

feldmarschall Model deserves credit for his skill in defending against 'Market-Garden', particularly given the state of Army Group B in September 1944, and for grasping at once the vital importance of the Nijmegen bridges. Although it is known as the Battle of Arnhem (or Arnhem-Oosterbeek to the Dutch), there is a case for calling 'Market-Garden' the Battle of Nijmegen, as some Americans have done.

In October 1944, Lieutenant General Brereton reported to General Marshall and General Arnold in Washington that 'Market' had been a brilliant success, which in his own terms was quite true. Lieutenant General Bradley attributed the defeat of 'Market-Garden' entirely to Montgomery, and to the British slowness on the 'island' north of Nijmegen. Major General Urquhart, who led 1 British Airborne for the last time to help liberate Norway at the end of the war, blamed the failure at Arnhem partly on the choice of landing sites too far from the bridges, and partly on his own conduct on the first day. Lieutenant General Browning's report blamed XXX Corps' underestimation of the strength of German resistance and its slowness moving up Hell's Highway, along with the weather, his own communications staff and 2nd Tactical Air Force for failing to provide air support. He also succeeded in getting Major General Sosabowski dismissed from command of 1st Polish Parachute Brigade for his increasingly hostile attitude.

Field Marshal Montgomery's immediate reaction to 'Market-Garden' was to blame Lieutenant General O'Connor for failing to deliver his expected miracle. On 28 September Montgomery recommended that Browning should replace O'Connor commanding VIII Corps, and Urquhart should replace Browning. In fact, Browning left England in November, having been appointed chief of staff to his old patron, Admiral Lord Louis Mountbatten, now heading South-East Asia Command. He rose no higher in the Army but became Comptroller of the Royal Household after the war. O'Connor left VIII Corps voluntarily in November 1944, having been promoted to command Eastern Army in India.

On further reflection, Montgomery blamed himself for part of the failure of 'Market-Garden', and Eisenhower for the rest. He also argued that the

▲ *Brigadier Gerald Lathbury commanding 1st Parachute Brigade, taken in Britain after his remarkable escape from the Germans following 'Market-Garden'. Recovering from his wounds under German guard in the St Elizabeth Hospital in Arnhem,* *Lathbury escaped with PAN help and led his party (including four American glider crew) back across the Lower Rhine on 22 October, being collected by storm boats of 506th Parachute Infantry Regiment. (IWM photograph H41640)*

salient along Hell's Highway provided a base for the attacks eastward across the Rhine in 1945, describing 'Market-Garden' as 90 per cent successful. Again, in Montgomery's own terms this was true, since the battle had forced Bradley to redeploy First US Army northwards and halt Patton. But, in October, Bradley placed Ninth US Army in charge of XIX Corps on the boundary with 21st Army Group, leaving First US Army with two Army Corps grouped around Aachen and a single Army Corps over-extended through the Ardennes forest to keep touch with Third US Army, which resumed its own attacks eastward in November. On 16 December the Germans took advantage of this error in deployment to launch their offensive through the Ardennes. The direct legacy of the Battle of Arnhem was the Battle of the Bulge (described in *Ardennes 1944*, number 5 in this series). On 28 December, Lieutenant General Horrocks, whose XXX Corps was being committed to the battle to support the Americans, suffered another collapse. Montgomery continued to protect Horrocks, sending him home to rest before returning him to XXX Corps for the final victory.

The next major Allied airborne operation, and the last of the Second World War, sought to rectify the faults evident in 'Market-Garden'. In Operation 'Varsity' on 24 March 1945, 1,696 aircraft and gliders landed 21,680 troops of US XVIII Airborne Corps under Lieutenant General Ridgway (17th US Airborne Division and 6th British Airborne Division), east of the Rhine as part of a river crossing by British XII Corps near Wesel. The whole airborne force landed in two hours barely 8km (five miles) ahead of XII Corps, which made contact on the same day. To the end of the war, 'Market-Garden' remained the only attempt by the Allies to use large airborne forces in deep penetration in Europe.

◀ *Paratroopers of 507th Parachute Infantry Regiment, 17th ('Golden Tallon') Airborne Division, boarding a C-47 Dakota for Operation 'Varsity' on 24 March 1945. By landing two complete airborne divisions (each with two, rather than three, parachute brigades/ regiments) in one lift, 'Varsity' became the largest and most congested single airborne drop ever mounted, larger than the first day of 'Market-Garden'. Although successful, it was also the most costly airborne drop ever mounted, with almost a quarter of the aircraft being hit or shot down by ground fire. Together with 'Market-Garden', this cast serious doubts on the future of airborne operations after the war.*

CHRONOLOGY

1944

13 August Montgomery suggests his 'single thrust' plan to Eisenhower.

16 August First Allied Airborne Army formed.

23 August Eisenhower gives priority to Montgomery's northern thrust.

26 August XXX British Corps starts its drive from the Seine.

29 August Third US Army starts to run out of fuel.

1 September Eisenhower takes command of the ground battle from Montgomery.

2 September Eisenhower adopts the 'two-thrust' plan.

3 September Browning threatens resignation. Von Rundstedt recalled to OB West. XXX Corps liberates Brussels.

4 September XXX Corps liberates Antwerp and halts. German First Parachute Army created under Student.

5 September 'Mad Tuesday' in Holland.

10 September Brussels conference between Eisenhower and Montgomery approves 'Market-Garden'. Guards Armoured Division captures 'Joe's Bridge'.

16 September First air attacks for 'Market-Garden' start after nightfall.

17 September D-DAY FOR OPERATION 'MARKET-GARDEN', THE START OF THE BATTLE OF ARNHEM. I British Airborne Corps, XXX Corps, XII Corps attacks start.

18 September Second airborne lift. VIII Corps attack starts.

19 September Third airborne lift. XXX Corps reaches Nijmegen.

20 September Assault crossing at Nijmegen. Main German attack on the Groesbeek heights.

21 September Fourth airborne lift. Germans recapture Arnhem bridge.

22 September Eisenhower abandons the 'Market-Garden' plan.

23 September Fifth airborne lift.

26 September Operation 'Berlin', the withdrawal of 1st British Airborne. **END OF THE BATTLE OF ARNHEM.**

5 October Last German attacks on the 'Market-Garden' corridor end.

7 October Allied air raids close Arnhem bridge.

27 November Last troops of First Allied Airborne Army leave the 'Market-Garden' corridor.

16 December The German Ardennes offensive (the Battle of the Bulge).

1945

4 February Germans destroy Arnhem bridge.

24 March Operation 'Varsity'.

14 April Allied liberation of Arnhem.

8 May V-E Day, the unconditional surrender of Germany.

A GUIDE TO FURTHER READING

Although the Battle of Arnhem was quite well known before 1974, it was largely Cornelius Ryan's book, *A Bridge Too Far*, and the feature film based upon it that brought the battle to a wider audience. Since then, there has been a small flood of books of varying quality on 'Market-Garden', together with the publication of intelligence sources and higher commanders' memoirs for both sides. Most of these books are not easily available outside specialist libraries, and a new full-length study of the battle is now needed.

GOLDEN, L. *Echoes From Arnhem*, London, 1984. A personal memoir from a survivor of Arnhem, full of technical information on the signalling problems.

HUDSON, J.A. *Out of the Blue*, Indiana, 1972. A scholarly account of the American airborne forces, starting with an outstanding case study of 'Market-Garden'.

KERSHAW, R. *It Never Snows In September*, London, 1990. An excellent account of the battle from the German viewpoint.

POWELL, G. *The Devil's Birthday*, London, 1984. Despite some flaws, the best account of 'Market-Garden' now available, with a good bibliography.

RYAN, C. *A Bridge Too Far*, New York and London, 1974. The classic, journalist's account of the battle, also with a good bibliography.

SIMS, J. *Arnhem Spearhead*, London, 1978. A 'worm's eye view' of Arnhem bridge from a private solider.

URQUHART, R. *Arnhem*, London, 1958 (paperback 1960). The British divisional commander's own account.

WEIGHLEY, R. *Eisenhower's Lieutenants*, Indiana and London, 1981. The higher strategy of the campaign in North-West Europe, with a good section on 'Market-Garden'.

THE BATTLEFIELD TODAY

The 'Market-Garden' area has not changed greatly since the Second World War, although there are more major roads and built-up areas. The main A67/E34 road now runs west to east from Antwerp to Venlo just south of Eindhoven, which is significantly larger than in 1944. Nijmegen and Arnhem have also grown in size, and both have rebuilt their town centres, which were heavily damaged in the fighting.

The starting place for visiting the Arnhem battlefield is the Airborne Museum at the old Hartenstein Hotel in Oosterbeek. Commemorative marker columns, some with a 'Pegasus' symbol, identify important sites on the battlefield. The road and rail bridges at Arnhem were rebuilt after the war. A new road bridge was opened in 1977 just west of the original bridge, which was renamed the 'John Frost Bridge'. The main A48 road now by-passes Arnhem to the east, also bridging the Lower Rhine, and leads eventually to Deventer, where the bridge over the Ijssel was used to represent Arnhem bridge for the motion picture *A Bridge Too Far*.

Along the Club Route, Joe's Bridge and the bridges at Grave and Heumen are still intact. Among the memorials to the 101st Airborne and 82nd Airborne are those at Son, Best, Veghel, and at St Anthony's Church at Breedeweg on the southern end of the Groesbeek heights. At Nijmegen a new road bridge has been built on the site of the old one, and the main features of the battle are easily identifiable.

WARGAMING ARNHEM

For the Second World War enthusiast, the attraction of 'Market-Garden' is that it has something almost of everything. It has high strategy, élite troops on both sides, airborne operations, assault river crossings, small-unit actions, armour *v.* armour battles, resistance fighters, supply convoys, weather factors, fighting on open ground, in wooded hills, and among houses, all within a self-contained battle lasting ten days. There is also much information available on the technical side, airborne forces and Waffen-SS being favourites with writers on uniforms and equipment, and with figure manufacturers. From this, and from several first-hand accounts, it is possible to discover or devise any number of challenging wargames scenarios.

Strategy Games

Starting at the top, the planning for 'Market-Garden' lends itself to the Committee Game, in which each player has his own personal role. This kind of game is often used in conjunction with a later operational game. All that is needed is a briefing sheet for each player, a table to sit round (and thump occasionally) and a set time-limit. For 'Market-Garden' the most interesting Committee Game is the meeting that never happened, between Eisenhower and his senior commanders after 1 September to thrash out strategy and supply problems, which may well result in the battle never taking place at all. As a more realistic alternative, try a meeting at 21st Army Group Headquarters on 9 September, with Browning and representatives from SHAEF and 2nd Tactical Air Force present. There are four options: to go on the defensive along the Albert Canal; to attack north-west towards Breda and Rotterdam clearing the Scheldt; to attack north-east towards Venlo and Wesel; or to carry out the historical plan. All have points both for and against them.

A variation on this is the 'Hidden Agenda Game' in which a player's main effort goes into fighting his own side while the battle goes on around him (perhaps a little unfair to the historical figures, but good fun). Montgomery wins if he gets Eisenhower to swing First US Army north of Aachen, no matter how badly his attack goes; or Model wins if he frightens Hitler enough to give him all the extra troops he wants. The Committee Game often leads to a Strategy Map Game, which can also be played by itself with at least one player a side, an umpire, and three identical maps of the area. Both players draw their dispositions and intentions, and the umpire tries to reconcile the results.

The Computer Wargame, which promised so much for the solo player a few years ago, has all but vanished as manufacturers have gone for graphics rather than realism. *Arnhem*, produced by Case Computer Simulations in 1985, is a solo game down to battalion level for the Allied player, and one of the best computer wargames ever marketed. There is also a 'Market-Garden' scenario in *Crusade In Europe*, produced by Microprose in 1985 as a solo/dual game at divisional level. Although issues of supply, weather and airpower have been left out, this is actually good, as it allows you to explore what should have happened by switching all your air support to 1st British Airborne at Arnhem and attacking vigorously with XII and VIII Corps to open up alternate axes. I usually manage to win by capturing 's Hertogenbosch and Utrecht before swinging east.

Operational Games

The classic approach to Arnhem at the operational level is the Megagame, a giant version of the Map Game with as many players as possible taking part, each representing a specific headquarters staff and ideally in a separate room. This gives ample opportunity for the representation of communications difficulties, particularly by using commercial baby alarms as radios - they have the right sort of unpredictability! A particularly fiendish game designer could construct an entire game for players representing the staff of I Airborne Corps switching radio channels and trying to establish what is going on.

In the only Megagame of Arnhem I have tried, Horrocks and Browning (admirably played by a former Parachute Regiment officer) won handsomely by keeping the Heart Route to Helmond open until the Germans collapsed, by taking the risk of dropping a brigade due south of Arnhem bridge in the first attack, and by holding back a reserve of one regiment/brigade for each airborne division in England with Browning himself until he could see where the enemy was. The conclusion on the historical plan, to quote the winner, was: 'It's not so much A Bridge Too Far, as Too Far From the Bridge!'

At the other extreme, it is possible to mount a very simple 'scissors cut paper' style game with three players, representing First Allied Airborne Army in England, 2nd Tactical Air Force, and the Luftwaffe, together with an umpire who decides the weather. The players draw up programmes for the day and announce them simultaneously, with the umpire moderating the results. If the two Allied plans do not conflict, the weather is not bad, and the Luftwaffe does not stop them, then the next drop takes place or XXX Corps advances with air support. The two Allied players are allowed to consult if they miss a day to do so.

Tactical Games

Most good commercial rules, such as WRG's *Wargames Rules 1925–1950* or the Firefly rules, have ways of simulating airborne assault, particularly at the common 5mm (1/300th) scale. The easiest way to mount a paratroop drop is to fly in a model Dakota (available commercially) on a stand and drop paper disks representing each figure or element from a determined height. Remember to allow for the effects of enemy fighters and anti-aircraft fire. A glider can be represented by a similar paper disk, or

by a paper dart thrown by the player, to be replaced on the table by a model. Allied paratroops landed with their personal weapons, but it took time for them to recover. Properly trained troops could drop their parachutes or evacuate a glider in less than 30 seconds, but a bad landing would knock them unconscious (at least) and a battalion needed about an hour from landing to making a formed attack.

A major attraction of 'Market-Garden' is the unusual mix of forces fighting on both sides, especially along Hell's Highway. Try Battalion 'Jungwirth's' action at Koevering with German paratroops and assault guns on one side, American paratroops and British armour on the other. The Germans win if they can hold any section of the road long enough to mine it properly. Particularly for the wargamer who likes unusual figures, Arnhem is one battle in which small fire-fights using larger 25mm (1/72nd) scale figures together with aircraft models can be very interesting. One scenario is a fight over a crashed glider (either scratch-built, or a deliberately sacrificed kit) with the player dicing for each occupant as he emerges.

Once on the ground, airborne troops have the worst of both worlds, with little firepower and not much mobility. The idea is to land where the enemy are not, advance to seize an objective, and hang on to it. One of the features of 'Market-Garden' was that, although both sides could be suppressed by heavy firepower, it was extremely difficult to move even small units physically off an obstacle. With figures, the defence of Arnhem bridge and the Oosterbeek pocket, or the assault crossings at Nijmegen and Heveadorp, are best wargamed as small unit actions rather than the whole battle (or you might try 2mm scale instead). Remember that, at 1/300th scale, Arnhem bridge, which was 650m long, would be more than six feet not counting the approach ramps! For boardgamers, the *Squad Leader* rules provide the basis for the game. Otherwise, as close and mixed a terrain as possible, with houses, rubble and trees, should provide a good game. A King Tiger tank should not be able to manoeuvre too freely, as the airborne troops have nothing that will stop it except at point-blank range. A reverse periscope, allowing the player to see from ground level, is useful for this kind of game.

Other characteristic features of 'Market-

Garden' are all-round fighting, and reinforcements for one side or the other arriving at unpredictable intervals. The best example of this is the Polish parachute drop at Driel – what would have happened if Sosabowski really had tried for Arnhem bridge again? Generally, any scenario should aim for a high level of uncertainty and confusion on both sides, with artillery and air support suppressing rather than destroying targets, and coordinated attacks being very hard to mount.